NOAH MAX

Conducting for a New Era

Noah Max

Good to meet a
fine musician.

Edwin Roxburgh

Conducting for a New Era

Edwin Roxburgh

With a foreword by Sir Andrew Davis

THE BOYDELL PRESS

First published 2014

The Boydell Press, Woodbridge
ISBN 978 1 84383 802 9

The Boydell Press is an imprint of Boydell & Brewer Ltd
PO Box 9, Woodbridge, Suffolk IP12 3DF, UK
and of Boydell & Brewer Inc.
668 Mount Hope Ave, Rochester, NY 14620–2731, USA
website: www.boydellandbrewer.com

A catalogue record for this book is available from the British Library

The publisher has no responsibility for the continued existence
or accuracy of URLs for external or third-party internet websites
referred to in this book, and does not guarantee that any content
on such websites is, or will remain, accurate or appropriate.

This publication is printed on acid-free paper

Designed and typeset in FF Scala and Scala Sans by
David Roberts, Pershore, Worcestershire

To my wife, Julie

Contents

Music examples

ix

Figures

I have in my library a very small number of books on conductors and conducting. Some of the earliest thoughts on the subject are to be found in Berlioz's *Memoirs*, which share with Leopold Stokowsky's autobiography a certain amount of highly entertaining imaginative fiction mixed in with the facts. From Sir Henry Wood's slim volume I remember advice on the importance of of labelling carefully one's three rehearsals suits (three-piece of course!) so as not to get them mixed up! Others offer valuable insights into the psychology of the relationship between conductor and orchestra.

Of the works that are concerned primarily with technical matters my most treasured are those by Hermann Scherchen and Max Rudolph. Edwin Roxburgh's new book, however, surpasses them all, especially for those of us involved in the performance of twentieth- and twenty-first-century music.

When the BBC Symphony Orchestra was formed in 1930 perhaps its most important brief was the commitment to the promotion of new works. During my time as Chief Conductor of that wonderful orchestra I conducted many premières (and some important deuxièmes!) of works by composers ranging from the internationally renowned to the just emerging. It was a fascinating and rewarding experience, but from the very beginning of my career twentieth century and contemporary music had constituted a large part of my repertoire.

I could certainly have used Edwin's help in those early days! But even now, in working my way through the very detailed examples in the book I have found myself marvelling at the clarity with which he analyses (and solves!) the problems which arise in these works and many like them. From the classic case of getting out of the 11/4 bar in *The Rite of Spring* to the complex interrelationships between tempi in Birtwistle, this book makes one constantly exclaim: 'But, of course, THAT's how you do it!'

For every conductor, from the aspiring to the highly experienced, Mr Roxburgh's Miraculous Manual is a must. But it will also prove fascinating reading to anyone interested in learning how a composer's intentions may be more perfectly realised and his performers enabled to make music with the greatest degree of security and comfort.

Andrew Davis

June 2014

□ □ □ □

Acknowledgements

In a book entirely related to copyright material I am very grateful to all the music publishers who have generously loaned copies of often huge scores for reference. Permission to reproduce examples from these scores has been kindly provided by all the publishers involved.

Examples 4–10   *Le Sacre du printemps*, Igor Stravinsky
© Copyright 1912, 1921 by Hawkes & Son (London) Ltd. Reproduced by permission of Boosey & Hawkes Music Publishers Ltd.

Examples 11–12   *Khorovod*, Music by Julian Anderson.
© 1997 by Faber Music Ltd. Reproduced by kind permission of the publishers. All Rights Reserved.

Example 13   *Suns Dance*, Music by Colin Matthews
© 1987 by Faber Music Ltd. Reproduced by kind permission of the publishers. All Rights Reserved.

Example 14–15   *The Origin of the Harp*, Music by Thomas Adès
© 1999 by Faber Music Ltd. Reproduced by kind permission of the publishers. All Rights Reserved.

Example 16   *Sal's Sax*, Joe Cutler
Reproduced by kind permission of Cadenza Music.

Example 17   *Paths and Labyrinths*, Music by Simon Bainbridge
© Copyright 2001 Novello & Company Limited. All Rights Reserved. International Copyright Secured. Used by permission.

Example 18   *Symphony of Three Orchestras*, Music by Elliot Carter
© Copyright 1976 Associated Music Publishers Inc. All Rights Reserved. International Copyright Secured. Used by permission.

Examples 19–20   *Pli selon pli (Portrait de Mallarmé) für Sopran und Orchester*, Pierre Boulez
© Copyright 1977 by Universal Edition (London) Ltd., London/UE 31747.

Example 21   *Jeux vénitiens*, Witold Lutosławski
Copyright © Mannheimer Musikverlag GmbH. All rights reserved. Reproduced by kind permission of Hal Leonard MGB.

Examples 22–3   *Preludes and Fugue*, Music by Witold Lutosławski
© Copyright 1972 by Polskie Wydawnictwo Muzyczne SA, Kraków, Poland. Rights for worldwide sales by consent of Polskie Wydawnictwo Muzyczne SA. All Rights Reserved. International Copyright Secured. Used by permission.

Example 24   *Giardino religioso*, Bruno Maderna

Examples 25–6   *Chamber Concerto*, György Ligeti

Examples 27–8   *Pneuma*, Heinz Holliger

Example 29   *De natura sonoris* No. 2, Krzysztof Penderecki

Example 30   Symphony No. 1, Krzysztof Penderecki

Example 31   *Atmosphères für Orchester*, György Ligeti

Example 32   Symphony No. 7, Op. 105, Music by Jean Sibelius

Example 33   *Inner Light I*, Music by Jonathan Harvey

Example 34   *Transfigured Wind II*, Roger Reynolds

Examples 35–7   *Désintégrations*, Tristan Murail

Example 38   *Tethys (from Saturn)*, Edwin Roxburgh

Example 39   *Valley of Aosta*, Music by Jonathan Harvey

For their unreserved goodwill in offering their views for Part Two of the
book I am indebted to Leon Botstein, Lamberto Coccioli, Lionel Friend,
David Hockings, Nona Liddell, Jane Manning, Anthony Payne, Julian
Pike, Ross Pople, Christopher Reed, Joel Sachs, Timothy Salter and David
Wordsworth. Peter Johnson and Ronald Woodley have given generous
support in providing funding from the Research Department of BCU
Birmingham Conservatoire UK. I am very grateful to Matthew O'Malley,
the studio manager of Birmingham Conservatoire, for producing the
DVD for Part One and for his expertise in editing the final format. I am
also indebted to Dreambase Studios for their friendly association in
producing the DVD for Part Three of the book. For their patience and
dedication in producing examples, figures and symbols in the text, I
owe a debt of gratitude to Stephen Mark Barchan and Jenny Roberts.
My gratitude also goes to David Roberts for his impeccable editing and
setting of the text. David Wordsworth also wins my thanks for dealing
with the logistics behind what has been a complicated project. Finally, I
wish to thank my wife, Julie, for her tireless support in helping to prepare
the type copy of the text.

Edwin Roxburgh
London, September 2013

Introduction

In the twenty-first century the world of classical music has evolved
into one of great diversity. Technology has opened the doors of cultural
experience on a scale which could not have been envisaged in previous
centuries. The facility to listen to music of our own choice at any
time of day or night is a great asset, but it cannot take the place of
live performances. Transferring the spirit of the concert hall or opera
house to a recording studio is an art in itself, as far as it is possible to
achieve a comparable representation of a live performance. But it is the
prerequisites of live performance which this book addresses, specifically
in the adventurous repertoire of progressive music from 1950 onwards.
Since then, the role of the conductor has become a more complex matter
in a cultural world of rapid changes and developments.

The labelling of artistic movements such as 'post-modern' or
'minimalist' cannot hide the fact that national musical identities
have been overtaken by the impact of the world becoming the 'global
village' which technology has created. Rapid communication has made
composers search more widely for a distinctive vocabulary which can
be fed by international rather than national characteristics. This wide-
ranging diversity of style and language is a challenge to conductors, who
must recognise the need for greater technical resources than were once
required.

In the nineteenth century conductors consistently performed the
music of their contemporaries. This was not the case in the first half of
the twentieth century, when many conductors achieved celebrity with
little concern to perform the music of their own time. The technique they
used to conduct a Beethoven symphony could be applied to Tchaikovsky,
Elgar and even to early Schoenberg, but not to Stravinsky. *Le Sacre du
printemps* created the need for a wider range of technical procedures,
especially in relation to irregular pulse, which became a hallmark of
the language of music and its evolution throughout the twentieth
century. The bitonal harmony of the work also required a more intensive
analytical capability in aural perception on the part of the conductor.
Schoenberg was equally demanding on the conductor's ear in *Pierrot*

Lunaire, but stayed with regular common time in simple or compound units.

The second half of the twentieth century found many more conductors being actively concerned in the promotion of new music – Hans Rosbaud, Paul Sacher, Pierre Boulez and Oliver Knussen, to mention a few. The repertoire they performed created a new art form in conducting which has even more relevance in the twenty-first century. This book is designed to explore the stylistic characteristics involved, the technique of the gestural language required, the aesthetic criteria and the aural perception which inform all aspects of rehearsal and performance. It is not widely appreciated just how complex these issues are, especially in relation to post-1950 music. There were no suitable courses for this repertoire available to students when Igor Markevitch underlined the need for radical revision of instruction for conductors by stating in 1954 that 'Before starting his career he (the student) should also have led the most significant contemporary works, with particular attention to those which are already part of the standard repertoire, such as *Le Sacre du printemps* ...' He continues: 'to those I would add Boulez's *Le Marteau sans maître*.'[1] Boulez was more trenchant about training needs: 'In the field of contemporary music, the conductors who come forward (students) have no training, which is not their fault, since the academies and conservatoires offer only a weak and often mediocre education in this area.'[2] In the twenty-first century there *is* concern for such training in many academies and conservatoires. The motivation for this book is a desire to feed that concern in establishing broad principles which can be applied by students and professional conductors who, like Bruno Walter, occasionally admit to technical inadequacy: 'How often my conducting technique has failed me when I was concerned with modifications of tempo on emotional grounds to which my gestures proved unequal!! ... supreme intensity of feeling will always take possession of the entire personality – thus, our emotional exaltation will diminish our attention to technical perfection, and on the other hand the striving for the latter will lessen our intensity; it is only *complete mastery* [my italics] that is able to reconcile these opposites.'[3]

Walter's statement was made in relation to his own repertoire, which was mainly classical and romantic, but included Ravel and Debussy at times. He died in 1962, but is still venerated in the twenty-first century. As a pupil of Mahler, he had a technique that was supple and adaptable to the vast range of expressive characteristics of his repertoire. Taking Walter as an ideal focus for the art of conducting in the first half of the twentieth century, let us consider attributes which must be added to a conductor's technique in relation to progressive composition after 1950: an aural perception which extends to non-tonal music; rhythmic perception which can control constant irregularity of pulse; the comprehension of a vast range of composition techniques unrelated to music prior to 1950; an understanding of the applications of electronics to ensemble and orchestral performance and an awareness of progressive design improvements and technical capabilities of instruments often implicated in the music of imaginative composers, especially in the explosion of hundreds of percussion instruments now exploited. A conductor who is unaware of these requirements will produce mechanical and dull performances of this repertoire.

The evolution of the art of conducting can be seen to rest on the shoulders of composer/conductors. Berlioz, Wagner, Mahler, Furtwängler, Maderna and Boulez, to mention a few, all considered composition as an essential attribute to conducting. As there are many notable exceptions to this view, such as von Bülow, Nikisch and Abbado, it is important to consider the responsibility a conductor adopts in conducting a première. The reputation of Mozart and Beethoven cannot be damaged by a poor performance, but in a first performance the living composer can be destroyed by an inadequate presentation. It is on this premise that the relationship between the study of conducting and composition has often arisen. Boulez declares that 'Teachers of composition and conducting ought to be in the same boat – and that is unfortunately not the case at the moment [2002], which I find disastrous.' He continues: 'This type of teaching aught to be essential, for one cannot separate the writing from the practice, as is generally the case.'[4] The importance for a conductor to study composition is stated strongly by a conductor of great distinction, Hermann Scherchen: 'The tuition [conducting] should comprise the most intensive practical study of composition. ... He [she] must learn to determine in each work, the inner dynamics according to which melody, harmony, rhythm and architecture are co-ordinated. Only thus will it become possible for him [her] to perceive the constructive principles of each individual work and deduce from the work itself the correct tempo, style and technique demanded.'[5] Furtwängler is equally firm on the need for a conductor to be able to compose in a very emphatic statement: 'If I have conducted, throughout my whole life I have done so as a "composer". ... Even if I attempted to point out and formulate some state of affairs, I did so as a composer, as a productive musician. That is my solid starting point in every case.'[6] The last sentence is of great importance. A conductor does not have to pursue a dual role as professional conductor/composer, but artistic conducting *does* require the perception of a composer in the realisation of a score. This is especially relevant in the preparation, rehearsal and performance of a new work. Without the trained aural perception which a composer should bring to an unperformed score, the conductor is at a disadvantage, as is the composer of the work.

The conclusion that can be drawn from these quotations is that conductors do not have to be composers in order to fulfil their function, but they must study composition to inform the artistry of their role. With this foundation the conductor's art in performing music of any era can be seen as focusing the subjective artistry of each player in an orchestra into a concentrated fusion of the expressive spirit of a performance. If this is absent the result is mechanical and superficial.

The added requirements for conductors that were mentioned above have a positive effect on a conductor's perception of the music of any period. This holistic approach is exemplified in Scherchen's work as a conductor. His repertoire was extremely wide. Unlike so many of his contemporaries he could adapt to the most progressive music of his time together with that of Bach or Tchaikovsky. While dispensing with a baton most of the time, his use of it was extremely eloquent. His courage in taking over the première of Berg's Violin Concerto at twenty-four hours' notice is also apparent in his recording of Beethoven's 'Eroica' Symphony at the very fast tempi of the composer's original metronome marks as a scholastic exercise. His contribution to the development of the technical requirements of progressive music well beyond his own lifespan is an outstanding record of dedicated achievement. Without a baton he was able to develop an expressive and clear communication of complex rhythmic structures in the music of such composers as Varèse, Nono and Xenakis. Dispensing with a baton completely, Boulez has also been hugely successful conducting the music of earlier generations such as Wagner, while brandishing a distinctive conducting style which is adaptable to the music of any period. Mahler's view that 'There are no bad orchestras, only bad conductors'[7] is a sweeping generalisation, but it does reflect something of the nature of the division which exists in the twenty-first century between conductors who understand the stylistic diversity of contemporary music and who can adapt their technique to the music of any era, as opposed to those who devote themselves to established classics at the expense of revealing new concepts in their programming.

In the early stages of studying the art of conducting I consider it to be of great value to use a baton and to develop a technique related to its use. This establishes the essential ingredient of economy together with the axis function of the wrist, elbow and shoulder, discussed in good text books on the subject. There is a school which denies the use of the wrist when conducting with a baton. This works perfectly well in standard repertoire before 1950 but would be a hindrance in the repertoire related to this book. As with fundamental principles of technique in any art form they have to be adapted to the individual practitioner. Physically we are all distinctive. But the wrist anchored to the baton will only work in the repertoire which created the concept. My own decision to abandon the baton was made the first time I conducted Schoenberg's *Pierrot Lunaire*. The hands seemed so much more adept at expressive gesture than the baton. That is a purely personal view and not meant as a determinant factor in the successful direction of a work. It is possible to emulate Scherchen's occasional use of the baton in appropriate works and dispensing with it in avant-garde music. But the complexities which inform so much music after 1950 create a need to revise traditional concepts to the point where consistency of technique without a baton is advisable. Therefore, this book relates entirely to a conducting technique without the use of a baton.

As with the music of any period in history the range of styles and categories in the repertoire since 1950 is enormous. In having to be selective I have chosen fields in which there are complex issues for conductors to consider. For this reason minimalist composers do not feature because the conducting requirements for such works are conventional and do not need explanation for a conductor who is practised in standard repertoire. But such composers as Messiaen, Maderna or Boulez occupy a complex world to which conventional conducting techniques require additional technical resources. The aim of this book is to offer solutions to the issues presented to conductors by such works. The observations and recommendations offered are by no means absolute. There are as many ways of conducting the music discussed as there are conductors. What is offered is one method which determines consistency in technique while supporting a subjective approach towards interpretation.

Part One is designed to establish technical principles (not rules) which formulate the relationship between musical perception and physical gesture. It is assumed that basic techniques have been established and practised by the reader, but it might be necessary for these to be reassessed. Once these concepts have been applied to contemporary music the conductor will have a much wider gestural vocabulary to inform and enhance a technique for the performance of music of any era. The works discussed to illustrate the application of the prescribed techniques cover a wide variety of composers and genres of composition.

The substance of Part Two is based on interviews with performers and composers who have had wide experience of performing contemporary music involving a variety of conductors. Having been an orchestral musician myself, I am conscious of how much can be learned from analysing an orchestra's response to both effective and ineffective direction. To have a variety of views on this issue can assist a conductor in making decisions about the responsibilities which accompany the art, both in performance and rehearsal.

For Part Three the reader should endeavour to obtain the scores for the works discussed. To gain the most from the text constant reference to the score is essential. With a subject so much related to physical gesture it is also necessary to have visual demonstrations of the techniques involved. For this reason this book is accompanied by a DVD to illustrate the application of the recommendations made in the text. While the tracks follow the course of Parts One and Three in the book, cross-referencing is not necessary. The visual examples should be viewed independently.

I have selected *Le Marteau sans maître* to exemplify the technical
characteristics required for all of the works analysed in Part Three.

It is hoped that the book can also be of value to composers in
assessing what is possible for a conductor to achieve in conveying graphic
complexities to an orchestra or ensemble.

PART ONE
Fundamental principles of technique

As the first Director of the Royal College of Music, Sir George Grove's motto for the institution was 'A player may be perfect in technique, and yet have neither soul nor intelligence.'[1] To appreciate the strength of that statement we have to define 'technique'. Essentially it is the mechanical aspect of an art form as distinct from its expressive characteristics. No matter what the art form, the interrelationship between technique and expression, each serving the other, is an absolute principle, regardless of the manner in which the substance is executed. We would not expect a violinist to play a Mozart concerto if the scales and arpeggios relating to the work had not been learned as a technical foundation separately from the artistic product.

The large number of books available which deal with the fundamentals of beating patterns and basic functions of pulse are useful as a starting point for the issues dealt with in this book. For its clarity and musicality in explaining basic principles my preference is for a volume published as long ago as 1933: *Handbook of Conducting* by Hermann Scherchen.[2] It has not been surpassed for its structured perception of technique and its application to the art of conducting. The present book takes Scherchen's foundation principles as a starting point for the extension of the technical requirements of a new age. It is also significant that Scherchen's distinguished reputation rests on his championship and conducting of the progressive music of his own time. While he rarely used a baton, his instruction in the book illustrates his own sensitive use of it. As an implement for developing economy in technique I consider it to be an essential element in the early stages of study. In eventually dispensing with it my own decision was based on a compulsion to use the expressive and supple use of the hand and wrist rather than the secondary implement of a 'piece of wood'. For a conductor who used one of the longest batons in history, it is interesting to read Adrian Boult's recommendation on this matter: 'There is no reason why anyone who wishes should not conduct without a stick [*sic*]. With small choirs and orchestras very beautiful results can be obtained in a way that could not be done if a stick were used, for the human hand is more expressive than a piece of wood.'[3]

When a baton is used it should always be chosen with a fulcrum point immediately beyond the bulb. Balancing it on the forefinger in see-saw fashion is a good way of checking this important feature (DVD track 1). A baton must have its own life in the hand rather than being a dead weight. The balance point between the first and second joint of the forefinger is an essential part of its fluency and its expressive function. A 45° angle across the palm of the hand governs the line of continuity from the arm. This diagonal angle is a natural position for creating a central focus for the beat. While Boult kept his thumb consistently on top of the baton he was able to perform the conventional repertoire of his own time with elegant assurance. But it was not a manner which could succeed in the rapid and varied displacements required for conducting the music of twentieth- and twenty-first-century avant-garde composers such as Boulez or Birtwistle.

The music stand

The position and height of the music stand will vary according to
the height of individual conductors. While it is important to try to
memorise scores this is rarely achieved (even with conductors who have
photographic memories) in the kind of works which are analysed in Part
Three. The conventional flat 90° angle of the stand encourages many
conductors to sustain a 'head-down' position when looking at the score.
In my experience as an orchestral instrumentalist this always gives the
impression of detachment from the orchestra. With complex works it can
leave the performers unaware of the characterisation of their individual
parts. In any circumstances and in any repertoire the conductor must
retain eye-contact with the players as much as possible. The head should
never be lowered to look at the score, only the eyes. Standing too close to
the music stand will automatically induce the head to bend downwards.
If the stand is angled upwards slightly from the 90° angle a suitable
distance will be established and the eyes can look down at the score
without the head turning downward (DVD track 1).

□ □ □ □

14 *Stance*

A 'stand-at-ease' position for the legs is modified by the right foot being slightly in front of the left, balancing on the heels rather than the toes. (As with all other aspects of technique, a left-handed person will interpret instructions in mirror-fashion.) This provides a central axis movement from left to right in focusing directions on various sections of the orchestra. It would be a dull conductor who makes this into a self-conscious rule, which we are all guilty of breaking by occasional digression from the basic stance. But awareness of the importance of an authoritative demeanour should always inform our movements. This basic stance is important for that reason.

The eyes play a very important role in the conducting vocabulary. In Part Two there are numerous observations from various performers who discuss this important issue. All conducting gestures should be focused in the central global space in front of the body and eyes of the conductor. Hands and eyes are then aligned for every single gesture (DVD track 1). If the beating is performed with bent, retracted elbows, the beats will be focused at the side of the body separate from the eyes. This divided focus is unhelpful and unclear. The position of the arms is, therefore, vital to all aspects of technique. Freedom from tension in shoulders and arms is the first consideration. Imagining the sensation of the arms floating on the surface of water provides a good analogy for freeing the forearm from tension. I offer a useful exercise to find a natural, relaxed suspension of the arms in preparation for the conducting process. With arms hanging naturally at the sides of the body, swing them backwards and forwards several times, making the arc gradually higher. Then allow them to stop at the base-line of the beat, level with the waist, with hands at a central point aligned with the eyes. Muscular tension must not occur at the landing-point. Now the arms will have established the natural extension-point for conducting. It is essential to keep the palms of the hands pointing downwards. This basic rule prevents the elbows from falling into the restricted position of closing into the sides of the chest. Turning the palms of the hands upwards while the arms are suspended will automatically draw the elbows into this restrained position (DVD track 1). A natural curve of the extended arms, with a base-line established at the waist, also provides a format for endurance in lengthy works.

Having played under Giulini's direction I can report that his beat base-line was considerably lower than the waist, even when conducting a chorus in Verdi's *Requiem*. It worked extremely well. He always sustained excessive arm extension. This underlines the important function of the elbow in the beating process. While the shoulder is bound to be slightly involved in the formation of the beat, it is the elbow which is the main axis for it. When elbows are bent too much and drawn into the sides of the rib cage, the mutual alignment of the eyes and hands is lost, so that the focus for the players becomes divided.

It would be a dull world without contradictions to resolve and paradoxes to unravel. Everything which I have recommended so far would have been dismissed by the great conductor Nikisch. Film footage of 1913 illustrates the legendary manner he used for 'mesmerising' players with his baton held high and level with his eyes. At that time, with a repertoire which never broke away from the confines of a single, even, time-signature, the choreographic focus could be levelled at any height to suit the individual conductor. That cannot be the case in the twenty-first century, with the repertoire under discussion in this book. Such a high base-line restricts the geometry and limits the activity to a window of one foot. It would be impossible to regulate the varying pulse units in *Le Sacre du printemps* in such a confined band of action. In the post-1950 world it would be even more impracticable. Today we need to use the large global space which our extended arms occupy in front of the body, where there is a vast number of angles available to conduct the complex music of the twentieth and twenty-first centuries. While explaining the impracticability of Nikisch's base-line in today's world, the 'mesmerising' eyes are another matter. The importance of sustaining eye-contact with the orchestra cannot be emphasised too strongly. Even with the need to use a score in so much modern music the importance of keeping your head out of the score is imperative. Karajan's habit of closing his eyes at rapturous moments seems rather self-indulgent to this writer. It implies self-absorption. This might not have affected the response of a distinguished orchestra like the Berlin Philharmonic, which recognised it as an eccentricity of their great conductor, but it does imply a distraction from the total commitment to the players and composers which the conductor's role demands. Ecstatic posturing is no longer acceptable to an intelligent orchestra. Such emotion is best demonstrated in Nikisch's intensity, not in Karajan's melodrama.

Having established the basic position for the arms at the outset of a piece or section, the manner of the beat, especially in so much modern music, is more complex than it might seem. It is a fallacy to imagine that the action of the movement from one beat to the next (the action, not the pulse) sustains an even speed. Taking a metronome mark of ♩ = 40 and repeating several downbeats with an even movement it will be discovered that the action looks like pasting or painting a wall! There is no pulse definition. The action needed for the beat is one which obeys a law of physics. A bouncing ball will gradually move slower towards the peak and accelerate when falling to the ground. This describes exactly how an effective and clear beat will work. In the absence of muscular tension the weight of the arm will create a natural acceleration towards the base-line and gradually move slower towards the peak, just like the ball. At the peak the ball stops before descending by gravitational pull at a faster rate than the ascent. Exercises can be used to achieve consistency in this approach towards beating. Establish a series of graded metronome marks, beginning with the very slow pulse of 40. Raise the arm to a peak level with the nose and let it fall by its own weight. At the base, start counting from 1 to 5. Following the action of the ball, which will stop at the peak before descending, don't allow the arm to fall until you have counted up to 5. With MM 50 perform the same exercise subdividing in 4 and descending on 4. At MM 60 subdivide in 3 and descend on 3. As the pace quickens the subdividing will be faster, so that by MM 70 the subdivision will be in a more rapid 4, descending on 4. This must be achieved without any sense of accent at the peak. A slight downward inflection of the wrist at the base will ensure safety of articulation because the players will sense the pulse in the immediate upward motion of the arm. This applies to the action at all dynamic levels (DVD track 2) as long as the 'bouncing ball' principle is followed.

It is easy to develop a common mannerism provoked by a conductor's attempt to drive the orchestra. The hand or baton arrives at the base half a beat too early, then punctuates the true moment of the beat itself with a jagged upward motion. This is disastrous in the context of modern music and must be avoided. Driving an orchestra can never succeed.

18 A conductor must *invite* response through fluent gesture and clear
Beating time units   direction.

The 'bouncing ball' principle is essential in controlling *rubato* or
constant changes of pulse in so much modern music. The acceleration of
the fall provides the most important element of conducting any kind of
music, that is, anticipation. For instance, it is possible to remain still at
the peak of a beat for any length of time before the acceleration of the fall
provides the anticipation of articulation in any circumstance.

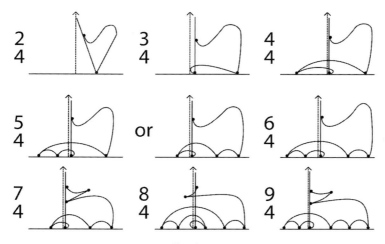

FIGURE 1 Beating gestures

Referring to the beating diagrams in Figure 1 we can now discuss
the manner of beating gestures. First, it is important to establish that
the expression 'preparatory upbeat' is to be abandoned. The constant
fluctuations of tempi in a work such as *Le Marteau sans maître* (especially
no. 4) cannot accommodate any kind of *preparatory* beat at any point.
Tempo has to be established by the *arc* of displacement between one beat
and the next. A preparation is required at the commencement of a piece
or section, but not a beat. Such a preparatory gesture requires only the
lifting of the arm from the base-line in time with the main pulse unit as
illustrated by the rising dotted line arrow in Figure 1. In a master class
Boulez once compared it to turning the ignition key in a car. The beating
diagrams emphasise the importance of arc shapes in the patterns. This
provides scope for expressive nuances and intricate rhythmic detail.

Consistent with the technique of any subject it is best to examine the
issues in slow motion at first. It is preferable to use a music example
rather than an academic exercise so that the artistic impulse is constantly
nourished throughout the process. The Prelude of Wagner's *Tristan und
Isolde* provides excellent material (Example 1).

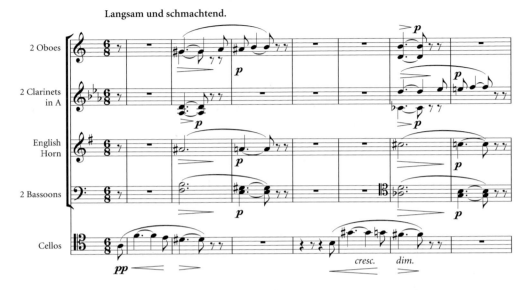

EXAMPLE 1 Richard Wagner, *Tristan und Isolde*, Prelude

It is a very slow 6/8 tempo beginning with the cellos playing on the sixth subdivision of the bar. Two issues arise for consideration. 1. Why has Wagner used a small, compound unit for such a slow piece? 2. How does the conductor beat the slow anacrusis for such a quiet opening?

The answer to issue 1 is that Wagner wished the performers to think of the pulse as two beats to the bar, not six. If he had used a crotchet unit rather than a compound to make it a 6/4 pulse, the line would lose its essentially sustained, flowing character which the compound unit implies. In explaining issue 2 we do have to refer to the 6/4 diagram in Figure 1 for the actual shapes of the subdivided 6/8 music. The preparation point for the anacrusis is at the far right on beat 5. Place the baton or hand at that point and simply raise the arm (as if taking a breath) in a perpendicular action to prepare the shape of beat 6 (Figure 2).

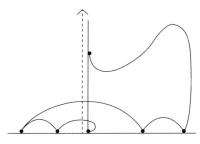

FIGURE 2 Subdivision of beats

It should be noted that all the upbeats in the diagrams in Figure 1 are
the same shape and at the same point against the central perpendicular
line – and always a little higher than the base-line. This consistency is of
great importance in establishing the technical resources for the works to
be studied. In conducting the Prelude to Wagner's *Tristan und Isolde* the
subdivision of the units will, of course, only be 'ghosted' with a floated
wrist action.

While considering the geometry of beating at a slow pace it is
important to establish further directional rules which are vital to slow as
well as to rapid tempi. The beating patterns in Figure 1 cannot signify
every nuance of shape for all musical gestures. But what becomes more
and more essential as the tempo increases is that at the base of the
beat in 3/4 and 4/4 time, the line must curve slightly in the opposite
direction to the ensuing beat, creating a small 'loop' action. In 2/4 time
the downbeat has to curve slightly to the right in order to make a suitable
preparation for the second beat. While these observations help to sustain
a fluent shape in a slow piece, it is of even greater importance at a rapid
tempo, when the geometry is mostly linear in shape and movement. This
is discussed in more detail in Part Three (pp. 195–7), with accompanying
demonstrations on the DVD (track 2).

Le Sacre du printemps is undoubtedly the work which opened a new era
in pulse structure. When it was first performed in 1913, composers
were already adopting irrational time units in some of their works: e.g.
Tchaikovsky's 5/4 movement in his Symphony no. 5, Holst in 'Mars' from
The Planets Suite. Important as these innovations were, the rapid tempo of
Stravinsky's 'Danse sacrale' created a new dimension in pulse for music
that was conducted. There was nothing new in the principle of irregular
units being used in music. The rhythmic structure of Latin syllables in
medieval plainchant sometimes fell into irregular stresses:

EXAMPLE 2 Peter Abelard, *O quanta qualia*

In the sixteenth century Claude Le Jeune was creatively involved in the
experiments deployed by French poets and musicians of the Académie
Française. One of his chansons was designed on the oscillation between
subdivisions of two and three, creating a variable metre:

EXAMPLE 3 Claude Le Jeune, *Le Printemps*

What was innovatory in *Le Sacre du printemps* was the requirement
of the conductor to use rapid signals of irregular pulse, which a large
orchestra had to respond to. It is puzzling that Monteux's colossal
achievement in conducting the première did not induce him to like the
work.

In the 'Glorification de l'élue' and in the 'Danse sacrale' from *Le Sacre du printemps* the constant oscillation between beats of two and three subdivisions requires a technical solution. Relying on the fundamental principles discussed it is very important to avoid the 'preparatory upbeat' syndrome. Simply lift the arm as if taking a breath with the main pulse value in mind. Control of the flexible units is achieved by varying the height of the beat of the two pulse values. It is useful to practise by simply deploying only downbeats at first. The exercise is governed by beating the main units (♩ ♩.) while articulating the varying subdivisions of each beat verbally. Putting this into practise at Stravinsky's metronome mark of ♩♩ = 144 in the 'Glorification de l'élue' it will be discovered that the dotted crotchet beat is considerably higher than the crotchet, and that the bouncing ball principle is especially noticeable as the dotted crotchet becomes much slower at the peak than that of the crotchet. While practising it is important to keep in mind that the players need to sense the varying pulse by anticipating the landing point of each beat. Such figurations as ⅜ 𝄾 ♫♩ are dependent on this spacing and the inevitability of the landing point which this gesture must provide. I have played in performances of this work in which the conductor has not varied the height of the beat, resulting in a lacklustre presentation devoid of rhythmic edge.

An added consideration which stresses the importance of the variable height principle relates to the preceding 11/4 bar with the hammered repetition of the same chord – *but* at ♩ = 120, and leading straight into the 'Glorification de l'élue' at ♩ = 144 (Example 4).

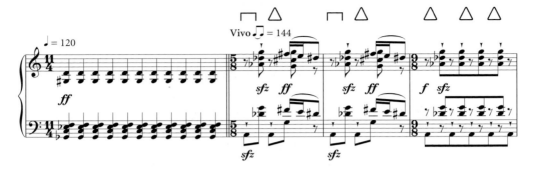

EXAMPLE 4 Igor Stravinsky, *Le Sacre du printemps*, 'Glorification de l'élue'

If this was a straightforward tempo change based on crotchet units only, lifting the tempo would not be a problem. The added issue is that the new tempo begins with a 5/8 bar in two. Stravinsky compounds the issue by notating the figurations and rests to indicate subdivisions of 3 followed by 2 (Example 4). Therefore, the first beat implies an initial slower pulse of ♩. = 96, much slower than the previous bar at ♩ = 120, in spite of the 'vivo' marking. My solution to this is based on two factors:

1   As the complete work is pivoted on syncopation of one kind or another, the ♪♫♩ motif will sound crisper if the beats are in the order of crotchet – dotted crotchet.

2   The pulse of ♩ = 144 can be established firmly with the immediate displacement of this new pulse arriving on the second beat of the bar. I would relate point 1 to the 9/8 bar as well, with syncopation dictating three dotted crotchet beats and not a four-beat bar of 2–2–2–3, which some conductors prefer. This creates 'um-pah' patterns, which are tasteless! Syncopation and diversion from regular pulse is quintessential to the whole work.

In the 'Danse sacrale' the constant irregularity of the strongly punctuated rhythmic structure makes the technique of varying height in the beating even more important (Example 5). By practising the geometric aspect of the beat with an exact replication in all the loop gestures of the final beat of each bar, the players will respond with confidence and assurance. A driving left-hand gesture on each *sforzando* will also maintain the dynamic contrasts required as the climax gradually builds in the coda.

This emancipation from a regular pulse had an enormous effect on the evolution of musical language in the twentieth century. The impact of this on the technical and artistic development of conductors has remained of primary importance to those who seek to support modern music. One of the first to adapt new technical resources to this revolutionary concept of rhythmic structure was Hans Rosbaud. By the simple expedient of establishing symbols to identify the quality of each beat, they could be placed above the stave to identify the values of each unit: ⊓ = one beat, two subdivisions, while △ = one beat, three subdivisions. From this simple formula complex rhythmic figurations can be adopted by a conductor to achieve a consistent geometric 'choreography' for each rehearsal and performance if planned in the learning process. The more complex the music becomes the more important it is to maintain this adaptable formula. The expressive characteristics which must accompany the technique will be discussed in individual works. As with learning a conventional instrumental work where fingerings have to be established early in the learning process, so the gestural language for conducting must be formulated initially in establishing the conductor's technical control of the ultimate artistic product. These symbols are an essential asset in establishing decisions made for the interpretation of a piece. In *Le Sacre du printemps* it is useful in the learning process to add these symbols to the score in the 'Glorification de l'élue' and in the 'Danse sacrale':

EXAMPLE 5 Igor Stravinsky, *Le Sacre du printemps*: beating irregular pulses: (a) 'Glorification de l'élue'; (b) 'Danse sacrale'

(a) $\frac{5}{8}$ ⊓ △ | ⊓ △ | $\frac{9}{8}$ △ △ △ | $\frac{5}{8}$ ⊓ △ |

(b) $\frac{2}{16}$ ⊓ | $\frac{3}{16}$ △ | △ | $\frac{2}{8}$ ⊓ ⊓ |

Note how in Example 4 the left edge of the symbol is in line with the beginning of the unit it represents in the score. This is especially important in works composed later in the century.

In spite of the innovations in the last two sections of the work, conventional conducting can be applied elsewhere. A few observations and recommended solutions follow.

There is no more famous a solo for the orchestral bassoonist than the opening of this work. I have been present in a performance when the soloist has insisted on playing the first bar without the conductor. The danger in allowing this is that the soloist might choose a tempo unrelated to the continuation of the section. While it is important to create a sense of freedom for this difficult entry, 'ghosting' a beat establishes a consistency of tempo. After the opening pause, lifting the arm from the base in preparation for the fall into the second beat gives the spacing required for the soloist. After the pause on the third beat, lift away gently to prepare the fall into the fourth beat. This allows the soloist to spread the triplet figure in the third beat at the slow tempo, making the entry of the horn in bar 2 secure. It is the clear anticipation of the landing of beats which gives the player an essential sense of space in the phrase. At the slow tempo of ♩ = 50 the bouncing principle is of paramount importance, remembering that the ball stops at the peak before falling.

In Stravinsky's sketches the bitonal chord (which is organic to the whole work) is very evident, but not a note of the Introduction appears for the simple reason that it had not been composed at the time of writing the sketches. It was the last section to be composed. The orchestration is by no means consistent with the rest of the work in that the large woodwind section is predominant, with cascading motifs against mostly sustained brass and strings with double basses in a *divisi* of six. It is a maze of polyphony. Many performances suffer from too loud a dynamic with such active motivic material developing towards the repeat of the bassoon solo. The glistening character implied in the orchestration can be enhanced by a conductor's rounded gestures, which encourage precision, but delicacy and a quiet dynamic at the same time. The transparent orchestration itself provides the gradual accumulation of volume.

Irregular pulse makes a brief anticipation in the 'Jeu du rapt' at number 41 in the score (Example 6).

EXAMPLE 6 Igor Stravinsky, *Le Sacre du printemps*, 'Jeu du rapt'

Taking the trombones as primary elements, Stravinsky's rests are appropriate for the beating patterns needed. While this defies the compound rhythmic structure of the strings' patterns, as long as the conductor is metronomic in relating the equal subdivisions of the quavers, this should not be a problem for them. Such incisive beating is also essential at number 70 in the score.

The bass drum and the guero are articulating cross-rhythms against the rest of the orchestra, and must be prominent. To achieve this balance it is now common practice to replace the guero with an old-fashioned metal scrubbing-board and a wooden scraper – an inspired solution by imaginative percussionists.

Rhythmic definition in a very slow context appears in 'Le Sage' which has a 4/4 time-signature (Example 7). The excessively slow tempo makes the rhythmic unison required from the contra-bassoon, timpani and solo double-bass difficult without great clarity from the conductor. *Thinking* a quaver pulse with the preparation ascent from the base at ♪ = 84 helps uniform rhythmic inhalation for the bassoons and contrabassoon 2, preceding the unison articulation at the opening of the section. Each crotchet beat should remain at the base for a quaver value; lift on the second quaver of the unit to prepare to fall on the next crotchet, and continue in the same way. While this has an element of subdivision, in essence the avoidance of an actual subdivided beat provides a clearer point of articulation when the main beat remains static at the base-line before the preparatory quaver lift follows. This procedure is also valuable for the strings in the final bar.

EXAMPLE 7 Igor Stravinsky, *Le Sacre du printemps*, 'Le Sage'

The tempo relationship between the 'Glorification de l'élue' and the 'Evocation des ancêtres' is a vital element in establishing the metric modulation implied in the score. Performances which ignore this relationship by slowing down at the conjunction of these two movements make the sudden contrast of tempo in the following 'Action rituelle des ancêtres' ineffective. The underlying pulse relationship between the 'Glorification de l'élue' and the 'Evocation des ancêtres' sustains the latter at a vital pulse of ♩ = 52. If this tempo is sustained, the contrasting pulse in the 'Action rituelle des ancêtres' emphasises the sudden static, ceremonial character required. Stravinsky is explicit in the notation of the cor anglais motif at the third bar, indicating that the very slow tempo is essential to accommodate this rapid motif, with its rhythmic independence. This is equally important for the effectiveness of the bass trumpet repetition near the close of the movement, but with notation which makes it slightly slower.

Stravinsky had considerable difficulty in deciding on some of the time-signatures in these later movements. Each edition of the work contains changes. The sketches demonstrate this indecision. In the third bar of the 'Glorification de l'élue' the sketches reveal the 9/8 bar in 11/8:

EXAMPLE 8 Igor Stravinsky, *Le Sacre du printemps*,
'Glorification de l'élue', bar 3: the 11/8 bar in the sketches

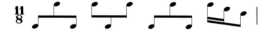

In relation to the sketches of 'Action rituelle des ancêtres' the cor anglais motif set against the alto flute solo is given to the bassoon. The sketches reveal many issues about Stravinsky's composing methods, even in his manner of orchestrating sections in short score. They make compelling reading for a conductor.

In approaching the 'Danse sacrale' at this ♩ = 52 tempo, it is essential to remain metronomic in pulse right up to the downbeat at number 142 in the score. This is all the bass clarinet requires to articulate the motif in the previous bar.

The beating patterns for the movement are shown in Example 5b above. Their application is shown in Example 9. A further important

EXAMPLE 9 Igor Stravinsky, *Le Sacre du printemps*, 'Danse sacrale' issue to underline relates to the varying angle of downbeats according to the number of beats in a bar, as discussed on p. 21. In the first section of this movement there are only two patterns, albeit with irregular values. There is either one beat to a bar or two. Because of the rhythmic unison involved, it is vital to distinguish between the perpendicular beat when one-in-a-bar and the angled beat when two-in-a-bar. This is even more important in the following episode at number 149 where a three-in-a-bar pulse is added. The three varying downbeat angles of each time-signature must be clear, not only for the benefit of those playing, but even more so for those counting bars rests. It is this section which has historic records of breakdowns in performance when a conductor has miscounted the beats in a bar and cannot recover.

Observing that all sections of the 'Danse sacrale' are marked ♪ = 126 is of great importance in capturing the ritualistic nature of the dance and its music. For anyone who has seen the film of Marie Rambert's re-creation of the Nijinsky choreography, with its stamping gestures and wild pirouettes of the 'chosen one', this issue will be obvious, especially at the final moment when Stravinsky brings the dance to a halting climax with a crotchet rest in 3/4 time (no change of tempo). The composer might have asked himself a question familiar to all composers: how do I end a piece which reaches such intensity and power? His choice of remaining in the augmented pulse of 3/4 requires exact metronomic judgement from the conductor, so that flutes sense the pulse for their rhythmic unison of quaver triplets, each divided into semiquaver triplets on the final beat of this bar. More silence! So many performances misfire on the final cadence at the close of the penultimate bar. Boulez's solution to making all the grace-note groups start at the same time and finish together on the final semiquaver of the bar is ingenious. By subdividing the final crotchet beat so that all the grace-note groups start on the subdivision (cancelling the dot on the semiquaver rest) the final semiquaver will be secure and heard clearly before the explosion on the downbeat of the final bar (Example 10).

A fitting end to such a galvanising ritual!

Of all the works which have influenced the evolution of the language of music in the twentieth century, *Le Sacre du printemps* stands supreme in establishing a new concept of pulse. Even the regular chord repetitions in 'Les Augures printaniers' invade a great number of film scores from the 1940s onwards, and it is not surprising to find the work featured in Walt Disney's *Fantasia* (1940). Another feature which opened the gate to the future was the use of a prominent percussion section. Four players are required together with two timpanists. As in a number of Janáček's works the piccolo tympanum is also used by Stravinsky. He was not alone in extending this element of the symphony orchestra. In *Daphnis et Chloé* Ravel uses six players on thirteen instruments, plus timpani. The skills of individual percussionists become more and more virtuosic so that the second half of the twentieth century found composers exploiting the medium with intensive concentration to the point where ensembles were created for percussion alone. Messiaen, Xenakis and others deployed the Strasbourg Percussion Ensemble in many of their works, often abandoning the need for a conductor.

Following the innovations in *Le Sacre du printemps* the deployment of irregular pulse evolved into quite complex applications throughout the twentieth century. Examples of these developments will illustrate the variations in the techniques already discussed in Stravinsky's masterpiece, especially in his use of the Russian *khorovod* (round-dance) in 'Cercles mystérieux des adolescentes' in *Le Sacre du printemps* It is the most potent application of this kind of rhythmic structure.

Julian Anderson has paid tribute to Stravinsky in giving the title *Khorovod* to one of his works. He has based it 'around the superimposition of different metres in several tempi simultaneously'. This occurs at the opening, governed initially by a regular time-signature of 2/2, combining differing rhythmic patterns. In the second section the conductor has to establish a beat of 5/16 ♩ ♪ = 80. Metric modulations then occur in 2/4 ♩ = 100, 3/8 ♩. = 66+. At the point where 6/16 (♩ = 66+) occurs, it is essential to beat in two (♪ = approx. 132) in order to accommodate the following 9/16 in four, with a triangle in the fourth beat. A series of 2/8 bars brings us back to ♩ = 100 in a bar. When a 3/8 bar is reached we can beat either one-in-a-bar at ♩. = 66+ or in three at ♩. = 150. Example 11 shows the pattern for practice.

EXAMPLE 11 Julian Anderson, *Khorovod*: beating solutions

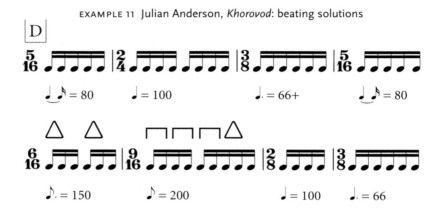

The important issue is that ♪ must equal ♪ throughout. In varying the height of the beat in the five differing rhythmic structures, the players will be secure in relating their music to the variations in the piece. It is very important to make the beating gestures look simple with a loose, flexible wrist action in the beat and a marked geometric shape in the direction of each beat, as in *Le Sacre du printemps*.

Another section in the work exposes similar issues. Example 12 shows a solution to directing the section at letter P in the score.

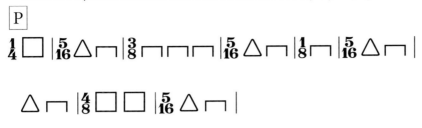

The square box represents four-semiquaver division of the crotchet at MM 135. Calculating the metronome marks of the other units is helpful in realising the choreography required of the conductor. 5/16 will be MM 117, but requiring two beats. The ♪. is MM 180 while the following quaver is MM 270. The 3/8 bar has the quaver at MM 270. 1/8 is the same. It is important to break down these metronome marks in order to decide how the conductor can indicate a beat at MM 270. An extended floating arm is essential. This acts as a rod to the wrist which must be able to direct the hand in a lateral swing whenever these units occur. Differentiating each quality of unit with size and direction of beat provides the clarity needed. Therefore, the 1/4 bar will require the largest action, the dotted quaver less high and the quavers in the 3/8 bar simply a triangle with no arm action at all. The number of beats in each bar varies from one to three. Keeping in mind the angle of each downbeat being in a slightly different direction (see p. 21) the repeated downbeat from the 1/8 bar to the 5/16 requires only a flick of the wrist in the 1/8 bar at ♪ = 270. It cannot be stressed strongly enough that any kind of tension is the worst enemy of such a passage. Before practising the mechanism proposed, the varying direction of each downbeat must be thoroughly digested, as illustrated in the accompanying DVD. The players are very reliant on the shape and clarity of each downbeat. Consistency in the manner of beating from one rehearsal to another is imperative.

It is reasonable to ask the question: why is such rhythmic complexity composed in such a challenging way? The answer is that there is no other way to convey the spirit of the idea which the composer imagines. In an attempt to simplify the notation of *Le Sacre du printemps* a conductor in the 1930s brought his own version of the 'Danse sacrale' to a rehearsal with the BBC Symphony Orchestra. It was transcribed into a regular

4/4 notation. To his great credit the leader, Paul Beard, refused to perform it. There is only one way to convey the rhythmic excitement of Anderson's piece, which is exactly what the notation implies. The jagged interruptions of regular pulse must be virtuoso in effect, just as in *Le Sacre du printemps*.

Similar rhythmic structures can be found in many late twentieth-century works such as Boulez's *Sur incises*. With rare exceptions in this work, no two consecutive bars have the same time-signature between pages 11–80, and most of them contain irregular units. The instruction to perform this very long section at *prestissimo possibile* should be interpreted in the interests of the performers, rather than the conductor. Boulez, conducting it himself, beats all records of speed! My own preference is for ♪ = 200. The comforting thought is that this is slower than ♪ = 270 in Anderson's piece! On the other hand it is a very long journey of concentrated fast conducting. One slip and the performance will break down. It is helpful to keep in mind that the extended loose arm is absolutely imperative in controlling the geometric shapes and their varying height in the irregular pulse.

Three points should act as a mantra for *Khorovod*:

1 Downbeats must always be in the centre.

2 Except for bars with one beat, all others must show the final beat in exactly the same motion, slightly higher than the base-line and contacting the perpendicular central line as a preparation for the downbeat. This is especially important when such a final beat is very short. Even the slightest delay with the landing of the downbeat will rock the players, who are also concentrating on the subdivisions of the irregular pulse.

3 Any tension will affect the clarity of the beating and will result in strain in such a long work.

A further issue in irregular pulse arises when a work in a rapid tempo requires subdivisions of a dotted quaver beat followed by a crotchet unit of four semiquaver subdivisions (Example 13).

$$\musDottedQuaver. = 152 / \musCrotchet = 114$$

$$\mathbf{\frac{9}{16}}\, \triangle\, \triangle\, \triangle\, \Big|\mathbf{\frac{4}{16}}\, \square\, \Big|\mathbf{\frac{6}{16}}\, \triangle\, \triangle\, \Big|$$

The first consideration is to recognise that each bar has a different number of beats. To control the exact displacement of a downbeat following a 4/16 bar the formation of the beat must become automatic. Using the three bars in Example 13 it is necessary to contradict the need for a higher position for the upbeat in the 4/16 bar, because it is now an extended duration in relation to the regular compound pulse. The height of the third beat of the 9/16 bar should be the basis for judging the rise of the 4/16 bar to a higher point, making the extended semiquaver automatic, landing precisely on the downbeat of the 6/16 bar. When you can discuss what you ate for breakfast while doing this exercise the automatic choreography will be secure – and it will be clear to the players. Once mastered, this makes the Stravinsky-like rhythmic patterns elsewhere in the work, seem easy, but not for the players. This is a remarkable work full of rhythmic vitality and contrapuntal complexity.

A further example of irregular pulse which extends the Stravinsky principle can be found in Thomas Adès's *The Origin of the Harp* for three clarinets, three violas, three cellos and percussion. The passage beginning at bar 70 in the score has the following time-signature relationships:

EXAMPLE 14 Thomas Adès, *The Origin of the Harp*:
addition of the double triangle symbol

$$\musCrotchet = 108 \qquad (\musDottedCrotchet. = 72)\ (\musDottedQuaver. = 144) \qquad\qquad (\musCrotchet = 108)$$

$$\mathbf{\frac{2}{4}}\, \square\, \square\, \Big|\mathbf{\frac{3}{8}}\, \triangle\!\!\!\triangle\, \Big|\mathbf{\frac{6}{16}}\, \triangle\, \triangle\, \Big|\mathbf{\frac{9}{16}}\, \triangle\, \triangle\, \triangle\, \Big|\mathbf{\frac{2}{8}}\, \square\, \Big|$$

I have added bracketed metronome marks and beating symbols to clarify analysis. The Stravinsky-style triangles require no explanation. As in the Matthews score the square box represents a four-division unit. The double triangle is used by Messiaen to illustrate an augmented single beat of six subdivisions. In the Adès score its augmentation relates to

EXAMPLE 15 Thomas Adès, *The Origin of the Harp*

the subdivision of three in the 6/16 bar, semiquavers being equal. In achieving absolute control of the speed variations in the pulse, the varying height of the units is the key to security. The Matthews piece demonstrated that any beat with more subdivisions than three is difficult to control because of its comparative length to two and three subdivisions. The practice method for the Adès is similar to the Matthews. Initially, the varying number of beats in each bar must establish the angle of each downbeat. The square box units establish the tempo and the height of this basic unit. The 3/8 subdivision unit must, therefore, be higher. It follows logically that the 6/16 units will be half the height. Articulating semiquavers while practising will also help to achieve the fluency required. Further on at bars 88–90 there is an added dimension to the subdivisions of the unit (Example 15).

I have added metronome marks to qualify the speed of each beat indicating that the one beat required for the 9/32 bar will be slower than each of the two beats in the 6/16 bar and therefore, higher in the lifting action. It is important to note in the 9/32 bar that the percussionist continues with a rhythmic motif consistent with the preceding 6/16, and that the note values in all parts are the same in both bars. The result is that the beating is identical to the fifth bar of Stravinsky's 'Glorification de l'élue', only faster.

When motor-rhythms are used by a composer, usually involving percussion, the repetitive motifs might appear simple for a conductor to control. But it can be deceptively challenging. This is especially the case when the basic pulse is uneven at a leisurely pace, as in Example 16.

EXAMPLE 16 Joe Cutler, *Sal's Sax*: motor rhythms

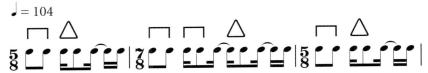

It is too fast for quaver beating, so the triangles become quite extended to ♩ = 69 in the larger beats. The players are totally reliant on exact displacement of the downbeat. Therefore, the varying height of the two units is especially important. As with any details of a score, the rhythmic structure must be accurately conceived. This is vital to the effectiveness of any work. If the conductor fails to enter the spirit of the music in this work it will be a dull mechanical performance, no matter how skilled the players.

Examples 11 and 14 show a breakdown of metric modulations in their related metres. Most composers rely on the single subdivision of a unit in such related pulses. A good example of a composer requiring absolute clarity of the issue is seen in Simon Bainbridge's *Paths and Labyrinths*. Example 17 shows the kind of metric changes set by the composer.

EXAMPLE 17 Simon Bainbridge, *Paths and Labyrinths*: metric modulation

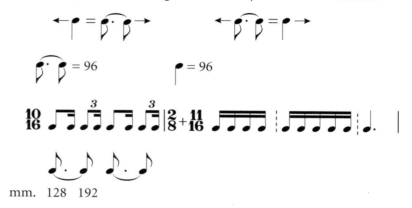

mm. 128 192

The composer's directions are placed above, while my own are below. Controlling such relationships in the beating depends on a clear calculation of the dotted crotchet equalling 128, which the composer wisely provides at the outset. The essential values in bar 1 add up to two main beats at MM 96, comprising subdivisions of ♪. = 128 and ♪ = 192. It is important to make these calculations because three instruments are playing in rhythmic unison with four different values in the main motif. Differentiating between the semiquaver and the triplet semiquaver is a distinctive feature of the phrase, which requires dissection in rehearsal in order to underline for the players this important difference. Breaking down the value of each semiquaver unit into metric values shows that a semiquaver equals MM 384, whereas the triple semiquaver division of the compound quaver equals ♪ MM 576. Therefore, the latter is shorter than the former. With the conductor beating the required two beats in the bar at MM 96 in order to sustain the metric modulation at the second bar, rhythmic unison will be achieved more easily if the triplet semiquaver is treated as a fast grace note.

The question arises, why has the composer used such complex notation? I suggest that it is for the same reason that Messiaen so often indulged the 'clipping' of a unit to establish the intensity of an irregular pulse. Bainbridge presents a *fortissimo* outburst in the first bar, which emphasises the rhythmic edge required in the phrase. My own preference would be to beat an irregular four, as in Messiaen, reverting to a crotchet beat undivided in the second bar. This intensifies the sudden contrasts implied, giving clarity to the rhythmic unison.

Metric modulation was a primary feature of late twentieth-century music. It is analysed in depth with Harrison Birtwistle's pulse piece, *Silbury Air,* in Part Three. It plays a significant role in the music of Elliott Carter, especially in *A Symphony of Three Orchestras,* which is dedicated to Boulez and the New York Philharmonic Orchestra who gave the first performance. Carter has paid tribute to his dedicatee by rearranging the orchestral forces (as in Boulez's *Figures – Doubles – Prismes*) into three individual ensembles. While the work retains conventional time-signatures, the varying metronome marks governing the pulse changes are complex. For example, in Example 18a, at bar 102, the number of calculations which have to be made are organic to all previous and subsequent metric changes.

EXAMPLE 18 Elliott Carter, *Symphony of Three Orchestras*:
irrational units in metric modulation

Example 18b shows an even greater number of numerical hoops to jump through in order to qualify the change of tempo from ♩. = 80 to ♩. = 72. For the conductor the difference between the two tempi is not difficult to determine. For the composer it is a necessary hinge in the structure of the work.

A conductor must form a conclusion regarding the need for such exact metrical control by the composer. The answer relates to all of Carter's music. It is extremely contrapuntal in its linear relationships and its motivic rhythmic structure. There is an ingenious skill shown in the way each section of this work is joined by the dovetailing which the sometimes complex metric modulation establishes. There are no 'full stops' at any point in this work until the series of explosive interruptions towards the close. Like Boulez, Carter likes to control every nuance and every detail in a composition. Here there is an intriguing union of this need between the conductor (Boulez) and the composer (Carter). The most telling example is at bar 224 where every beat of each bar in a *molto accel.* section has a metronome marking: 5/4 ♩ = 54 ... 63 ... 75 ... 88 ... 103 ... 120. Carter's reason for such a measure is to secure the counterpoint of the motivic material with the punctuation of each beat. With this understanding a conductor must ensure that each beat is regulated as strongly as possible by metronomic accuracy. A practice method is to check the metronome mark of 54 with a metronome, then to set it at 120 without the sound, just the light giving a pulse. Close your eyes and conduct the whole bar with a steady accelerando then open them at the downbeat of the second bar to see approximately if your pulse relates to the pulsing light at 120. I don't consider this to be an elementary exercise in relation to a work which depends so much on pulse accuracy to achieve its textural character. The 'bouncing ball' principle takes on a different application in this context. If the ball is left to its own devices after the initial throw the phasing effect will be as illustrated in Figure 3a.

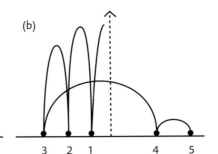

(a)

(b)

3   2   1   4   5

FIGURE 3 Control of exact metronome marks in varying tempi

As the impetus of the fall wanes, the pulse phasing of the bounce becomes faster. Figure 3b shows how this can be applied to conducting Carter's accelerating 5/4 and subsequent bars. Once mastered, the interpretation of the music can be addressed on a firm technical basis, the most important element of which is that each instrumental part should be played in a soloistic manner, even when marked *ppp*. The vitality of the music is in the expressive shape of the phrases, not simply in correct rhythmic displacement of figurations. Without the expressive content the music can easily become a crowded succession of notes rather than the brilliant colour-mixing and sweeping strokes of the composer's ideas. It is also good to find him using the correct spelling of *lo stesso* rather than the still current, but archaic form *l'istesso*.

☐ ☐ ☐ ☐

So far the issues of technique and pulse have been discussed only in relation to the right hand. (Left-handed conductors will make the appropriate mirror interpretation.) It would be dogmatic to prescribe technical procedures for the left hand. Of all characteristics in conducting, this is an element which should relate entirely to the body language and character of individual conductors.

There are many good conductors who mirror-beat most of the time. Their performances in standard repertoire prove that this can be a positive approach. This cannot be said of the requirements for the music central to this book, especially those works analysed in Part Three. Mirror-beating at a rapid tempo with an irregular pulse divides the attention of players from the central focus of the conductor's beat and eyes. The function of the left hand has parallels with standard repertoire in relation to cueing, emphasis and characterisation. But there is a case for being able to perform those functions when beating with the right hand alone. I witnessed a good example of this in my first post as principal oboist in Sadler's Wells Opera (now ENO) when Sir Colin Davis was the Director. He arrived at a *Sitzprobe* rehearsal with all the cast and orchestra present and asked us to allow him to practise by keeping his left arm behind his back throughout the rehearsal. It was impressive and successful. He did not use his left hand at all. I recommend this as a good test for the capability of any conductor. The work in question was Gounod's *Faust*. However, it has to be said that this exercise could not succeed in works by composers such as Carter or Stockhausen. But the principle of keeping the arms independent was very much in the mind of Davis, even in standard repertoire. Providing an independent use of the left hand creates a wide range of gestural vocabulary to induce variations of colour, characterisation, expression, dynamic inflexion, vitality and calmness; all of which enhance the effectiveness of a performance.

Freedom from tension in the arms is absolutely essential in any circumstance. It is also the foundation for developing independence of each arm. A good test for measuring is to practise beating three with the right hand against two in the left, using standard shapes. This ability is an essential requirement in performing a section of Michael Jarrell's

Trace-Écart. In preparing a performance of this work I had mastered the technique required, but in the first rehearsal I arrived at the page where the division of hands arose without having worked out how to turn the pages while my arms were occupied with activating differing pulses!

An even more complicated arrangement arose when I was composing my *Concerto for Orchestra*: a section required the conductor to beat four with the left hand against five in the right. With the patterns in Figure 4, I practised with the shapes required until it became automatic. Absorbing a graphic image of the geometry of the opposing shapes, acts as a memory guide to the physical function.

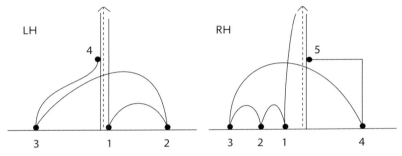

FIGURE 4   Precision in conducting differing units
at the same time with each hand

Remembering my oversight in Jarrel's piece, the five pages of score requiring this arrangement were set in a short score version on one loose page placed on a separate stand during the performance.

The independence of each hand becomes an even more complex issue of technique in 'Don', the first movement of Boulez's *Pli selon pli*. It becomes a graphic element of the score in the original version.

Boulez's concept of this work was to assert '[a method] of 'breaking up' or 'exploding' the unity of the group and then restoring it'.[4] Example 19 shows a section of the original score which illustrates this idea. With the restrictions on rehearsal time to explain how things worked Boulez was led to recompose the score in a definitive format (Example 20). The first version was conceived before the technique to conduct the work was calculated. Its improvisatory nature was bold in imagination, as the graphic structure of the original score demonstrates. I consider it

EXAMPLE 19 Pierre Boulez, *Pli selon pli*, 'Don' (original version)

Très libre, irrégulier
<u>Très hésitant, pour commencer</u>

Les signaux des différents groupes
sont complètement indépendants.
La réalisation ne devra pas forcément

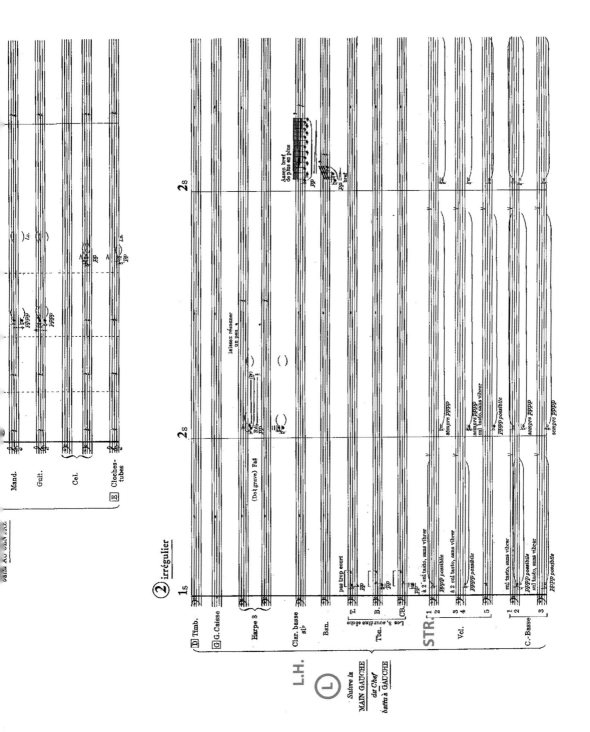

EXAMPLE 20 Pierre Boulez, *Pli selon pli*, 'Don' (revised version)

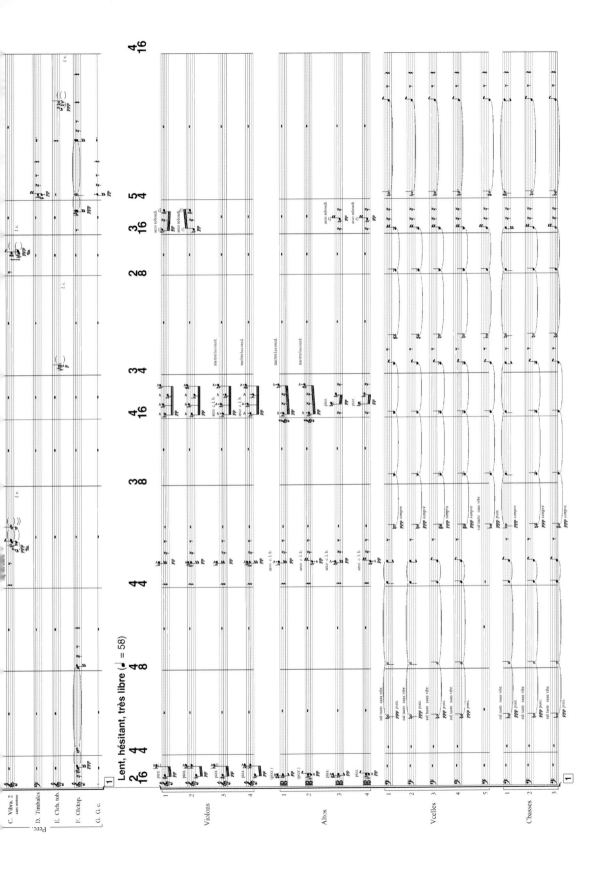

essential for a conductor to study the first version in order to understand the motivation behind the composer's concept of the work. Responding to my own inquisitive streak, I found it impossible to resist the temptation to perform the original version to discover the essence of such a bold adventure on the part of Boulez. With the gift of a substantial rehearsal schedule and Jane Manning as vocal soloist, the performance of all five movements of *Pli selon pli*, including the original version of 'Don', took place at the Royal College of Music, with brilliant playing from the students.

The following discussion of the original version of 'Don' illustrates how far a conductor can adapt to a new concept, no matter how complex. Boulez divides the orchestra into three separate ensembles. This arrangement requires the conducting signals to be placed in three different positions: far right, far left and (as the composer indicates) either the left or the right hand controlling the central ensemble. My own additional indications show an interpretation with the left hand operating the central signals. The upper ensemble in the score is controlled by the right hand with irregular numbers of beats (or signs, as Boulez indicates in the time-signatures) which I have marked in circles to distinguish them from the left hand signs. These are indicated with arrows. The right beats, while irregular, must relate to occasional variations of basic tempo, especially in bars with 4s signatures. In order to clarify the placement of left hand beats in the central ensemble, I have angled the arrows to indicate conventional shapes for each one. Left hand arrows, where the hand must signal to the far left for the lower ensemble, are represented with comparatively longer stems than the signals for the central ensemble. I have given them further qualification by placing a ringed capital 'L' below these arrows. In the first of the 2s bars of the lowest ensemble the players can judge the second beat in their parts as an upward preparation with the left hand for the downbeat in the following bar. With these individual displacements for the beats, practice should be done with each hand separately at first, to digest the geometry of the gestures, before application to the musical needs. When practising both hands together it assists the development of independence of hands by beating regular actions before attempting specific values and relationships.

The instructions which Boulez supplies underline the importance of mobility in the displacements of motifs. While he rejected the 'chance' methods of Cage, *Pli selon pli* explores improvisational characteristics related to chance, but only in the creation of slight mobility in the displacement of events within the texture, which are thoroughly and organically composed. Essays in Boulez's *Orientations: Collected Writings*, provide illuminating discussion on how the poet Mallarmé influenced the structural and aesthetic motivation behind the music. He explains that 'the words "*pli selon pli*" are used by the poet to describe the way in which the mist, as it disperses, gradually reveals the architecture of the city of Bruges'.[5] This image explains the static character of the music, *pli selon pli* (fold upon fold). Regularity of pulse can have no place in the texture. The three elements of substance require relative displacements, but with mobile interlacing of the articulations. Boulez asks for, not *p possible*, but *pppp possible*.

The atmospheric nature of the music is unmistakeable and it must be demonstrated in the character of the conducting. While the complex gestural language has to be consistently explicit, the manner of the beating should reflect an aesthetic understanding of the poetic implications. There is no better work to study the technique involved in developing independence of hands in expressive gestural demeanour. No instrumental manual can regulate this quality. It is implicit in the body language of individual conductors, once the technical aspects have been determined and absorbed.

Separating the function of each hand in 'Don' has relevance to general considerations on their independence. The most effective conductors use the right hand, with or without a baton, to direct as much of the musical content of a work as possible, no matter what period or style. Even the coda of *Le Sacre du printemps* benefits from a conductor using only the right hand in the *piano* bars, so that a strong attack, adding the left hand in the *fortissimo* and *sforzando* interjections adds force and assurance for the players to make powerful statements contrasting with the more restrained articulations in the section. As the *fortissimo* grows, both of the hands will help to sustain the intensity.

The *Oxford English Dictionary* defines 'aleatory' as 'dependent on the throw of a dice, dependent on uncertain contingencies'. John Cage explains the concept of 'chance' in his *Music for Piano* as 'operations channelled within certain limits (which are established in relation to relative difficulty of performance) – derived from the *I-Ching* are employed to determine the number of sounds per page'.[6] The process is to use a pencil on transparent pieces of paper, applying the result to a master – page, tossing a coin to determine clefs, using *I-Ching* possibilities to determine categories of notes and keys, then applying all of this to freedom in performance of time length, silences, duration of notes and their dynamics. While avoiding any mention of Cage, Boulez describes this kind of process as 'puerile magic'.[7] His own application has been discussed in relation to a concept of improvisation and mobile elements in *Pli selon pli*. A conductor is entitled to an opinion on either composer, but might find him/herself having to conduct works by both of them. In such circumstances judgement must remain private.

The period 1955–65 shows many composers experimenting with serendipity in various ways, some taking Cage's direction, others that of Boulez. But one in particular took a highly distinctive approach. In the programme note to his *Jeux vénitiens* (1961) Lutosławski discusses his own version as 'the loosening of time connections between sounds'.[8] He sees this as an 'enrichment of the rhythmical side of the work', giving performers the scope for 'free and individual playing' in an ensemble. He is careful to underline that the 'chance factor' is not the leading one to influence the way a composition is constructed, no matter how this will make each performance slightly different. Like Boulez, he puts the composer in control of events, not the performers, as in Cage. The distinctiveness of his technique is the comparatively simple form of notation which avoids virtuosic demands from the performers. Lutosławski rightly observes that many of his contemporaries who used his solutions to aleatoric techniques tended to be concerned only with rhythm,[9] the organisation of time and timbres and never, or very rarely, the organisation of pitch. He considered this to be the 'most important thing of all, without it, controlled aleatorism loses its meaning'.

With these observations in mind a conductor can get to the heart of Lutosławski's language. The fact that he often conducted his own works is reflected in the graphics of his scores, in which the conductor's role is illustrated clearly. In a chapter relating to conducting his music in general, he explains that the guiding role is restricted to rehearsals, and at the concert he confines himself to giving signs, signalling the beginning of the *ad lib.* passages while the rest plays itself. These guidelines relate to the first two movements of *Jeux vénitiens* with clear instructions in the score. The third movement requires intensive counting by the players in that there are no solid bar lines, only letters pursued alphabetically up to W, which the conductor indicates with the right hand. While recommending the left hand for cues at and between each letter, the issue of simply doing a downbeat at the demarcation can be unsettling for players by, say, the possibility of mistaking H for I. There are many scores produced in this period where random beats are illustrated by a sea of arrows in which no clear demarcation exists. My solution to this is that the conventional geometric shapes of 3 or 4 beats relating to a series or arrows can be put in the parts, so that the players can see exactly which arrow is being indicated at any time. The third movement would also benefit from such a procedure, as would the opening of the fourth. Fifty-four one-beat bars are played before a demarcation point is reached. It could be said that such a situation is present in the first movement single beat bars of Beethoven's Fifth. The difference is that Beethoven's music is motivic while Lutosławski's is not. Therefore it is more difficult to identify in bar displacements. At bar 54 Lutosławski deploys a graphic characteristic which relates to his perception that the guiding role of the conductor is related more to rehearsals than performances. Most of his conducted works rely on right hand arrow signals which introduce each entry of specified instruments, which then pursue their material free from the conductor's control. Example 21 shows how complicated this can become.

My recommendation is that rehearsal time will be saved if the entries are illustrated by the conductor shaping the arrow entries in a series of constantly shaped 3 or 4 beats marked in the parts.

The use of arrows combined with conventional beating is taken to a new level of invention in Lutosławski's *Preludes and Fugue,* for thirteen

EXAMPLE 21 Witold Lutosławski, *Jeux vénitiens*

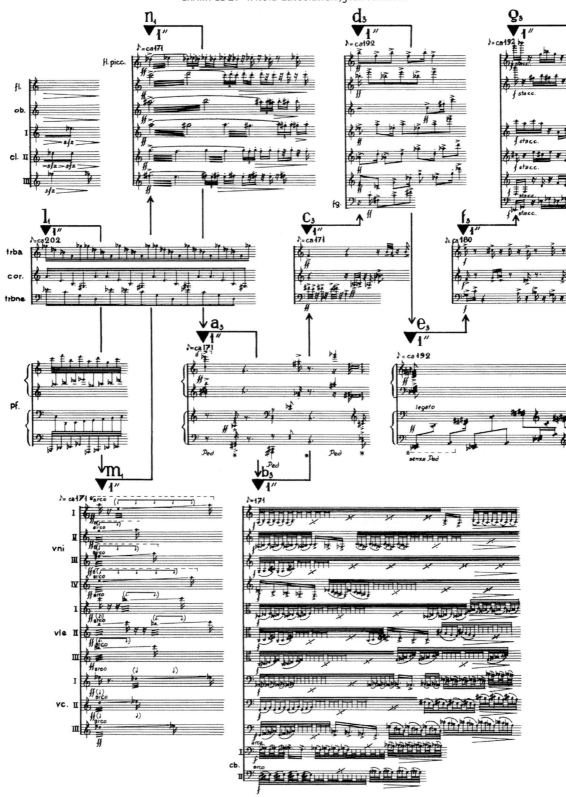

solo strings. It is also structurally innovative in that the seven preludes interlock with each other in a dove-tail manner. The composer specifies that they can be played in the written order if all of them are included in the performance. If a shortened version is used a smaller number can be performed in any order chosen by the conductor. In *Jeux vénitiens* the arrowed cues are white. These are also used in the preludes in aleatoric sections. Where the pulse becomes regular within these sections a black arrow is used. Prelude 6 deploys the combination of black and white signals while indicating the *sostenuto* element in the texture; the black signals control explosive rhythmic interjections making the two layers of substance into a vital conflict. This is a good illustration of the spirit which informs the conducting technique established for the work.

The Fugue introduces a further arrow symbol which takes the form of half an arrow. Its function is related to the manner in which the individual parts are printed. The fugue subject enters at figure 1 and is repeated by the cellos and viola 3 until figure 5. Within this section the subject or answer of the fugue enters three times. Using a left hand signal for these entries is an ingenious resource for sustaining the essential freedom of the individual parts. The nature of this freedom is illustrated in the opening statement (Example 22) where three instruments play the subject simultaneously but unsynchronised, especially if the expressive dynamics are exaggerated.

The twelve-note structure is a device for chromatic lines rather than a nod to Schoenberg.

There are copious notes in the score which explain the procedures clearly, except for the omission of an instruction for left-handed conductors to mirror the beating indications with confidence that the distinctiveness of the individual function of each hand will be understood by the players. Metronome marks are sometimes indicated without the conductor controlling the tempo. Establishing the pulse for each player separately in rehearsal is essential.

EXAMPLE 22 Witold Lutosławski, *Preludes and Fugue*

There is an issue in Prelude 2, in which a regular pulse is given by the conductor followed by an unusual metric modulation:

EXAMPLE 23 Witold Lutosławski, *Preludes and Fugue*, Prelude 2:
aleatoric conducting techniques

This is a rather elaborate way of slowing down the pace for the 5/4 bars, so it is useful to deduce that the crotchet in these slower bars is ♩ = approx. 125. These pulses alternate twice with strong rhythmic implications in the music, which are essential to the musical idea. The concept of creating complex contrapuntal music with un-complex means was a remarkable achievement for a composer, whose independence from the dominant influence of Darmstadt separated him from the mainstream *avant-garde* of the 1950s. Deploying the conductor in a role often remote from pulse beating was not unusual at the time, but Lutosławski's technique gave the art of conducting an entirely new and distinctive function.

While Darmstadt was primarily a hothouse for young composers, the presence of the conductor Hans Rosbaud at the courses was an inspiration to those, like Boulez, who also became distinguished conductors. Bruno Maderna was one of the most accomplished composer/conductors who graduated from this arena as a powerful voice in the promotion of new music. He was so much in demand as a conductor that his copious output as a composer (at the time of writing) was inadequately prepared for publication. In his monumental work *Hyperion,* eleven percussionists are requested, one of which plays only one articulation in the whole work. This is the kind of oversight for which an editor is required. Sadly, his untimely death in 1972 has left his *œuvre* mostly in his own beautiful manuscript. Aleatoric aspects are used in many of his works, containing explicit instructions for the conductor.

EXAMPLE 24 Bruno Maderna, *Giardino religioso*

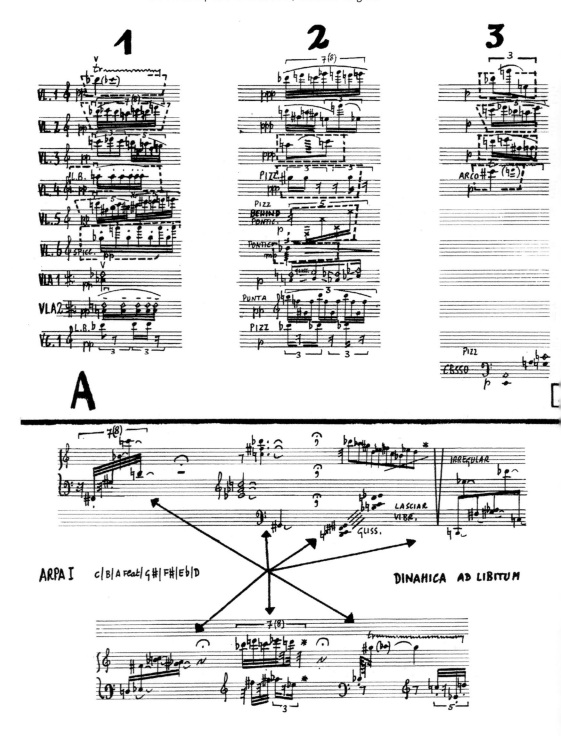

4 **5**

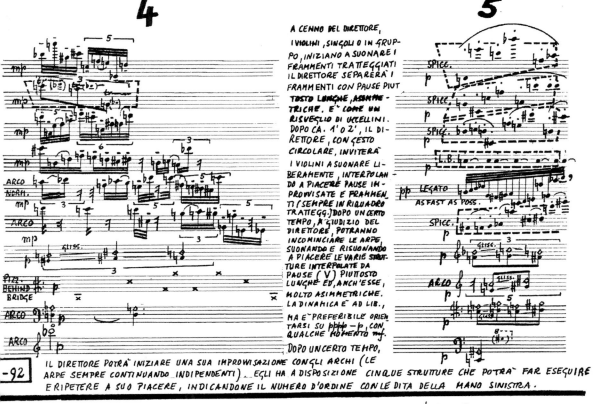

A CENNO DEL DIRETTORE,
I VIOLINI, SINGOLI O IN GRUP-
PO, INIZIANO A SUONARE I
FRAMMENTI TRATTEGGIATI
IL DIRETTORE SEPARERÀ I
FRAMMENTI CON PAUSE PIUT
TOSTO LUNGHE, ASIMME-
TRICHE, È COME UN
RISVEGLIO DI UCCELLINI.
DOPO CA. 1' 0 2', IL DI-
RETTORE, CON GESTO
CIRCOLARE, INVITERÀ
I VIOLINI A SUONARE LI-
BERAMENTE, INTERPOLAN-
DO A PIACERE PAUSE IM-
PROVVISATE E FRAMMEN_
TI (SEMPRE IN RIQUADRO
TRATTEGG.) DOPO UN CERTO
TEMPO, A GIUDIZIO DEL
DIRETTORE, POTRANNO
INCOMINCIARE LE ARPE,
SUONANDO E RISUONANDO
A PIACERE LE VARIE STRUT-
TURE INTERPOLATE DA
PAUSE (V) PIUTTOSTO
LUNGHE ED, ANCH'ESSE,
MOLTO ASIMMETRICHE.
LA DINAMICA È AD LIB.,
MA È PREFERIBILE ORIEN-
TARSI SU ppp—p, CON
QUALCHE MOMENTO mf.
DOPO UN CERTO TEMPO,
IL DIRETTORE POTRÀ INIZIARE UNA SUA IMPROVVISAZIONE CON GLI ARCHI (LE
ARPE SEMPRE CONTINUANDO INDIPENDENTI). EGLI HA A DISPOSIZIONE CINQUE STRUTTURE CHE POTRÀ FAR ESEGUIRE
E RIPETERE A SUO PIACERE, INDICANDONE IL NUMERO D'ORDINE CON LE DITA DELLA MANO SINISTRA.

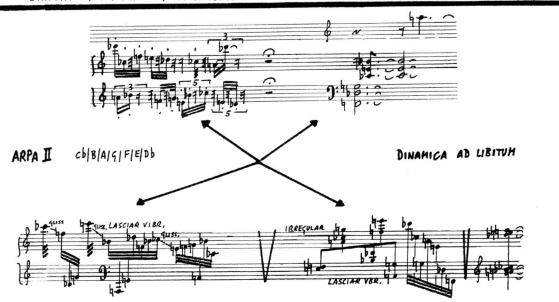

ARPA II   cb|B|A|G|F|E|Db   DINAMICA AD LIBITUM

Example 24 shows part of the first page of *Giardino religioso*. The landscaped format of the score at 64 × 47 cm is utterly impractical. No music stand exists that can accommodate the two-page spread of 128 cm. My own solution is to erect five standard orchestral stands with sections of cardboard 50 cm high spread across them. A further hindrance is that it is a loose-leaf score. With care, the arrangement proposed makes the use of this unwieldy score manageable in performance. The only reason for taking such trouble is that it is an excellent piece of music. It will be seen that the improvisation material is all notated. It is the superimposition of each motif which formulates the orchestration of the piece. The composer's instructions dictate how the conductor is to assert this control. It is useful to enumerate the procedures in short headings after the information has been digested:

1 Start individual groups.

2 1′–2′ ⌒: improvisation signal.

3 Cue for harps.

4 Strings improvise – left hand fingers indicate 1234 or 5.

5 Stop.

These tabulated instructions simplify the principle events to be signalled. My translation of the Italian instructions in the score relates to my enumeration of the signals required.

1 At the conductor's signal the violins, single or in groups, imitate the fragmented sketches. The conductor will separate the fragment with rather long pauses, which should vary in duration. The composer says 'it is like the awakening of a little bird'.

2 After 1′ or 2′, the conductor makes a circular gesture, inviting the violins to play *ad lib.*, interpolating freely, pauses, improvisations and fragments (always in relation to the sketches).

3 After some time, at the guidance of the conductor, the harps can be introduced, sounding and resounding at pleasure, the various structures interpolated between pauses (V) rather long

and, also to be very asymmetrical, the dynamics to be *ad lib.*,
but preferably *pppp – p*, sometimes *mp*.

4 After some time the conductor will initiate one of his
improvisations with the strings (the harps always continuing
independently). He/she has five structures available which can
be played following and repeated as he/she wishes, indicating
the order of numbered sketches with the left hand fingers.

5 The last instruction requires a recommendation from the author
to indicate any number between 1–4 with fingers, only adding
the thumb for figure 5.

Similar characteristics are used in other works of Maderna. When
transferred to a large orchestra in *Grande aulodia* the reconstituted
disposition of players into several individual chamber groups prepared
the format for each group when divided into individual improvisatory
ensembles. The conductor's role here is to choose a selected order of
the numbered improvisation events. As in similar works the conductor
must prearrange all decisions regarding the order of events so that the
textural result sounds through-composed and not casual. The question
might be asked: why didn't the composer make a definitive version of the
improvisations and interrelationships of the ensembles? One answer is
that in post-serial composition times the Darmstadt composers tended
to rebel against their initial desire to systematise musical language to
a ruthless extent. Improvisation became a leavening spirit for further
experimentation, which opened new fields of imagination. In this work
Maderna creates polyphony which replaces single line counterpoints
with ensemble groups in textural discourse. The variable relationships
between the groups can vary from one performance to another,
depending on the choices made by the conductor. It is an idea not
dissimilar to works of Boulez in the same period, where 'improvisation'
appears in some titles.

The intricate signalling which so much aleatoric music requires
from a conductor can hide the essential expressive character behind the
graphics. This is especially true of Maderna. In *Grande aulodia* the details
of dynamics, phrasing, articulation and quality of tone are abundant. In
rehearsing a work of this kind it is wise to break down each section of

the orchestra to direct each element separately. It is vital to be meticulous in obtaining the subtlety of texture which the details imply. With an orchestra that is unfamiliar with a composer's music, such detailed rehearsal helps the players to learn the piece in such a way that they are able to contextualise their own parts in relation to the whole, as they do in more familiar standard repertoire. In other words, they get to know the whole piece and not just their own parts.

While the word 'aleatory' has been coined for works containing substance which have a chance element in the graphics, there are many which use such free elements, but defy the strict meaning of the term. Common usage has come to associate it with indeterminacy and improvisation as well as graphic illustrations in a score.

But there are many composers who deploy aleatoric substance while retaining traditional forms of notation. Karlheinz Stockhausen's *Zeitmaße* is an example of this. It is studied in depth in Part Three. In his *Kammerkonzert* György Ligeti employs a similar combination of standard notation allied to a pulse with aleatoric *senza tempo* cadenzas deviating from it. Sections that are barred are under the control of the conductor. Ligeti chooses to use quite complex motivic material, which is designed to avoid any sense of accentuated pulse. The conductor's task is to sustain the pacing of the fluctuating rhythmic counterpoint in applying the composer's instruction that 'bar lines serve only to synchronize the parts; bar lines and bar subdivision never indicate accentuation'. He also requires 'very gentle' articulation from the wind. Paradoxically, these are characteristics I have in mind when performing so much music of Brahms. Example 25 shows Ligeti's process. The magic of the resulting texture is enhanced by the very quiet dynamics.

Page 68 in the score introduces a stream of arrow signals to indicate note changes for each instrument. Ligeti recommends constant downbeats with the right hand, using the left to indicate numbers for specific beats. The author's recommendation to employ the thumb last when five digits are required is reflected in Ligeti's caution over the use of the fourth finger. He enumerates the beats with I, II, III and V. As this is specified in the parts the system must be addressed. It does, however, present a problem. Both hands are in constant use, and there are three page-turns involved! My solution to this is to signal the beats with the

EXAMPLE 25 György Ligeti, *Kammerkonzert*

*) Siehe Fußnote Seite 8

) Picc. **pp = Pf. **pp**

***) Es ist egal, ob Vn. 1 oder Vn. 2 die Figur zuerst beendet (oder ob beide gleich-zeitig enden).

****) Es ist egal, ob Picc. oder Pf. die Figur zuerst beendet (oder ob beide gleich-zeitig enden).

*) See footnote, p. 8

) Picc. **pp = Pf. **pp**

***) It makes no difference whether Vn. 1 or Vn. 2 finishes its figuration first (or wheter they both end together).

****) It makes no difference whether Picc. or Pf. finishes its figuration first (or wheter they both end together).

right hand in conventional four-beat patterns leaving the left hand free for cueing and page-turning. Using a single-handed signal where possible in aleatoric substance is much clearer and more helpful to the players than divided gestures.

The rapid repetition of grace notes for up to one minute in this section might require an artistic solution from the conductor. Ligeti's instructions take into account that breaths will need to be taken by woodwind and brass players. He also accepts that rapid-tonguing capability will vary from one instrument (and indeed player) to another. Brass players and flautists will automatically prefer to double-tongue – a technique which is facile when the mouthpiece of an instrument is against the lips and not inside the mouth. With the mouthpiece inside the mouth, oboists and clarinettists have more difficulty in double-tonguing. It is quite common to find excellent players of these instruments who have not mastered the technique. Single-tonguing is no substitute in a passage of such length. In this kind of situation a conductor must accept a slower reiteration with more breaths taken by players of these two instruments, making sure that they never take a breath at the same time – as with Ligeti's own instruction. History reflects this dilemma. When Rossini visited England in 1822 for a production of *The Barber of Seville* he brought his own oboist who was expert in double-tonguing. This opera and many famous overtures of Rossini demonstrate the appeal this characteristic had for him. Example 26 shows Ligeti using a simple form of added-note values in sustained chords.

In relation to the way the parts are written it is useful for the players if the main units are beaten conventionally, but adding the quaver unit in the opposite direction to the final upbeat, as in Example 26.

It cannot be emphasised strongly enough that beating time is the least important concern for the conductor in this kind of work. Ligeti's instructions for the players indicate that the delicacy and gentleness of the expression is of paramount importance. The fact that most of the work is extremely quiet (*pppp* at one point) is indicative of the atmospheric warmth implied most of the time. If a conductor is too preoccupied with simply beating time the players will find it difficult to respond to Ligeti's expressive intentions. There are no rules to specify how a conductor should convey the character of such music, but the

EXAMPLE 26 György Ligeti, *Kammerkonzert*

*)Individuelles morendo in Picc., Clar., Clar. basso: die drei Spieler können – je nach Atemvorrat – den Ton verschieden lang halten.

*) Individual morendo in Picc., Clar., Clar. basso: depending on breath capacity, each of the three players can sustain his tone a different length of time.

choreography must show a floating quality, which caresses the base-line using rounded gestures to invite a non-accentuated response from all of the players. It is essential to demonstrate one's own perception of the beauty of such texture by inviting the response of each player's subjective artistry in mutual artistic endeavour.

☐ ☐ ☐ ☐

The term 'extended instrumental techniques' applies to works which involve what were once unorthodox forms of sound production and articulation on various instruments. For woodwind this includes over-blown harmonics, flutter-tonguing, slap-tongue, quarter-tone production, glissandi, alternative fingerings for varying tone colours and multiphonics on all instruments. There are also specific characteristics for individual instruments which will be discussed. For brass these extended elements include slap-tongue, flutter-tonguing, quarter-tone valve or slide positions, speaking into the tube and sometimes playing at the same time and multiphonics. The strings were more exploited than wind instruments in extended characteristics by composers in the nineteenth century. While Salvatore Sciarrino has composed works with extremes of harmonics in the twentieth century, style apart, these were equally deployed by Paganini and others in the nineteenth. After 1950 we can add the use of high natural harmonics produced at the extreme scroll-end of the fingerboard, fingered quarter-tones and playing on the tailpiece. The piano, harp and percussion take on a vast range of subtleties which constantly open new doors of imagination for the composer.

The bibliography lists several books by instrumentalists which explain extended techniques on specific instruments. They, and any other sources of information on the subject, are essential reading for a conductor. The main issue in preparing such scores is that it is not always possible to imagine the sound that will result from a prescribed notation. This is especially the case with the way in which a fine composer like Heinz Holliger notates a multiphonic for the oboe:

EXAMPLE 27 Heinz Holliger, *Pneuma*: 'extended' wind-instrument techniques

The instruction reads: 'Fingering as for B natural, e-hole open'. The player will, no doubt, produce a correct reading of the resultant

multiphonic, but lacks the pitch notation in the score to check if it is absolutely correct. For the conductor it is even more uncertain. While this is an anomaly in the composer's graphics it does not detract from the imaginative artistry which informs its context in the orchestral texture. The conductor has to find a solution. Initially, there is no case for misunderstanding on the part of the instrumentalist because the sounds from all the instruments relate to breath – the Greek title of the piece. There are clear directions for conducting. All the questions relate to the notation and instructions for production of unorthodox sounds. All woodwind instrumentalists play without reeds or mouthpieces, articulating consonants onto the crook or slapping the tongue against the bassoon crook's aperture to produce a 'popping' effect. 'Slap staccato' can be produced on the flute but on the oboe, clarinet and bassoon only without the reed. As an oboist I took great pleasure in playing the introduction to Monteverdi's *Orfeo* without a reed, in trumpet fashion. It gave a warm cornet tone – and a very astute conductor either ignored what I was doing or failed to notice.

The pianist uses a plectrum to 'stroke' the strings inside the piano. (A piano technician will insist that the plectrum should be made of plastic not metal.) The brass play what are described as diaphragm accents, inhaling and exhaling into their instruments without tone. (The use of the word 'diaphragm' is misplaced because it is a muscular membrane dividing the thoracic cavity from the stomach muscles, which are the real activating agent.) After all the winds are drawn into forms of slap-tongue articulations at bar 64, the reeds and mouthpieces are inserted into the woodwind instruments to set a new texture. The notation dispenses with traditional staves, dividing each instrument into three differing registers. It is important to imagine the effect of extremely random pitches avoiding diatonic triad intervals played very *staccato*, but intensely quietly in all the woodwind and brass. At this point the independence of each hand becomes a necessity for the conductor. For 30 seconds there are no bar lines. During this period the left hand directs the woodwind while the right hand is allotted to the brass. In varying phases independently of each other the hands direct differing dynamics, progressively introducing irregular accents until the page in Example 28 is reached.

EXAMPLE 28 Heinz Holliger, *Pneuma*

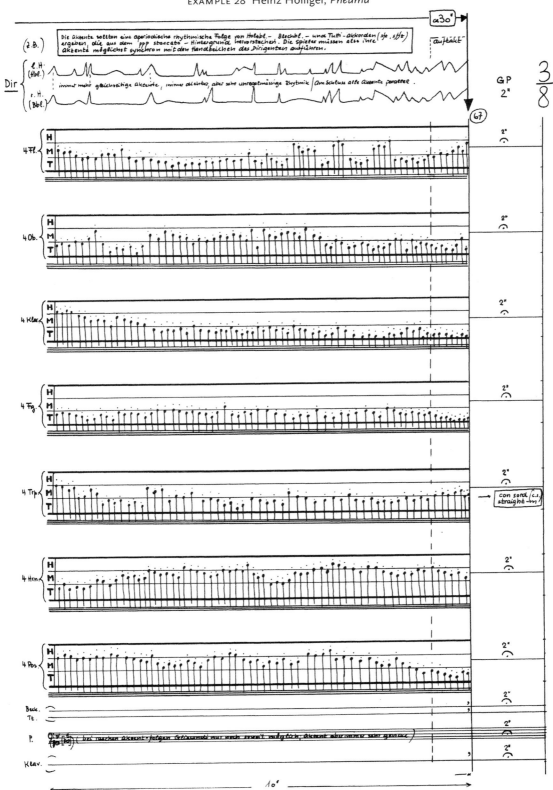

The instruction to the conductor reads: 'The accents should result in an irregular rhythmic sequence of woodwind, brass and *tutti* chords (*sfz, sffz*), which stand in relief against the *ppp staccato* background. The players synchronize the accents they play as closely as possibly with the conductor's signals.' For the players to respond to the separate hand signals it is vitally important for the conductor's arms to be completely free from tension. When the independent gestures become faster the 'bouncing ball' principle becomes ever more important. The players must be able to anticipate the moment of the accent in the normal way. A jabbing action will fail to achieve the rhythmic unison required. The culminating effect when both arms move in unison in the last few seconds is very exciting if the conductor enlarges the shape of the beat at this point.

For a conductor who is unfamiliar with extended techniques this score might seem disconcerting at first glance. But study is assisted by the copious notes and instruction which Holliger provides. Another important factor is that it takes a considerable amount of rehearsal time for the following reasons. Players will need to be coached in sectional rehearsals with no more than two instrumental groups at a time: flutes and oboes, clarinets and bassoons, horns and trumpets, trombones and tubas, piano and all percussion, recorders with sho and melodicas. The reason for organising rehearsals in this way for such works is for the benefit of the conductor as well as for the players. For the première of a more conventional work the conductor can recognise every sound in the score during the learning process. This is not the case where extended techniques go beyond conventional instrumental sound. Holliger is meticulous in the instruction provided for each sound-production, so that the players have an assured starting-point for preparation. In rehearsal, first efforts will create some amusement. The conductor's task at this point is to analyse the manner of production with each instrument, aiming at a refined tone and precise articulation, avoiding any random displacement and inconsistency of tone. As the instrumental techniques become more assured the conductor can digest the resultant texture and build the essence of the score in his/her mind with each rehearsal and stage of preparation. The players themselves will provide expert assistance when interrelated requirements are specified. An example of this is where the trombones are asked to place cor anglais reeds inside their mouthpieces, in crumhorn fashion. The cor anglais player will scrape the reeds appropriately thin for easy vibration and instruct the trombonists to soak them in water before the rehearsals and concert.

It must be kept in mind that the piece is a requiem for the composer's mother, breath being the defining element of life. It is a sensational work of art in which all aspects of the techniques involved create a highly imaginative sound-world even when the apogee of the sound of expelled air is reached with the bursting of a balloon which punctuates the closing chord.

'Extended techniques' has become a label to which I take exception. It segregates works which involve progressive elements from the mainstream. All great music in history has been created by composers who have *not* subscribed to current fashions in their own times. J. S. Bach was by no means a child of his time in creating the chromatic complexities of many of his works. The fact that the only works of his that were published in his own lifetime were the last three, indicates the general neglect his music suffered. Mozart's works became more and more chromatic in his later years, avoiding any association with the popular *stile galante*. Beethoven, Wagner and Schoenberg were innovators, creating music which extended current boundaries associated with the constantly developing capabilities of instruments. Exploiting such resources was integral to their compositions. Composers who deploy these constant developments have been a natural element of the evolution of musical language until the second half of the twentieth century when the label 'extended techniques' was attached to any work which contained a multiphonic or new characteristic of production. This label has been a useful weapon to any instrumental teacher who is too lazy to move with the times. I have even heard the nonsensical statement from a teacher who I respect in other ways, that any technical characteristic beyond the requirements of early twentieth-century music can be damaging to a student's playing. Holliger's example as an oboist defies such a mistaken assumption. The continuing development of the woodwind, brass and percussion families provides a constantly widening vocabulary for composers to draw on. It is essential for a conductor to study this wide range of instrumental capabilities to ensure that adventurous composers, such as those under discussion, are represented in their repertoire. While there are some composers who limit their vocabulary exclusively to sound production unrelated to any music before 1940, such as Helmut Lachenmann, there are those, like Holliger, who sustain a broad vocabulary which embraces all the characteristics which history has created for us. This is especially important in the need for a conductor to nurture the beauty of tone which is often required in the widening range of tone and textural qualities of, say, multiphonics. A player who attempts the production for the first time might sound like a beginner on the instrument. Once control is achieved the massed ensemble texture of multiphonics in the coda of *Pneuma* can be achieved. A *pp* dynamic in all the woodwind is intensely beautiful if the sound of the instruments is produced with Brahms in the minds of the players.

Quality of tone is equally important in the strings repertoire after 1950, which takes the section into unexplored territory. A seminal work from 1961 is Krzysztof Penderecki's *Threnody to the Victims of Hiroshima*, in which a string orchestra produces a catalogue of textures comprising non-specified pitches, bowing behind the bridge and on the tail-piece, plus striking the upper sounding board with finger tips. When required to bow *on* the bridge the large section produces a rather ghostly effect. The quarter-tones required are not quite so innovatory. Once the symbols for the notation have been digested, conducting directions can be determined.

Penderecki devises a novel way of reducing the number of staves required for divisi strings in *De natura sonoris* no. 2. Example 29 shows how he reduces twenty-two divided violins to one stave simply by numbering each player in a cluster glissando. The whole of the string section is involved, emerging from a dream-like opening for the *flauto a culisse* (pan pipes), a harmonium sustaining a high cluster, while crotales are resonated by a bouncing metal beater and a thunder sheet played with the hand. The conductor must imagine the rather peaceful character which these unusual articulations create.

EXAMPLE 29 Krzysztof Penderecki, *De natura sonoris* No. 2

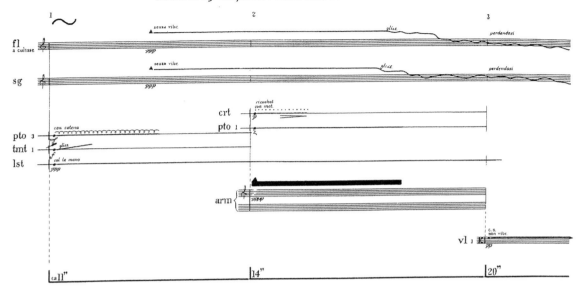

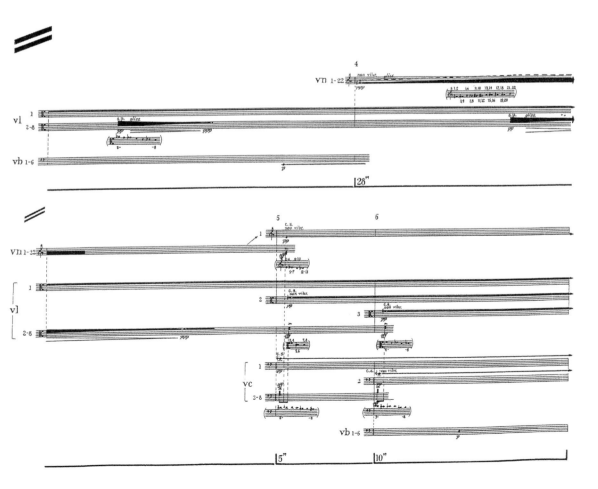

EXAMPLE 30 Krzysztof Penderecki, Symphony no. 1

*) Glissando beginnend mit dem höchsten Quartflageolett
   Glissando beginning with the highest fourth - flageolet
**) Glissando dort fortsetzen, wo vorher aufgehört.
    Please continue glissando at the point where stopped before.

The numbers above the score indicate constant downbeats from the
conductor. This can create difficulties if a player loses count of the bars
before an entry. Penderecki solves the problem in his Symphony no. 1.
Downbeats are replaced by small groups of beats with conventional
shapes designated by integers. Example 30 indicates how clear this
is for the players. The large arrows are two-handed signals, while the
half-arrows indicate left-hand beats, as in Lutosławski, which are to be
conducted with conventional shapes. The group glissandi in the violins,
created on artificial harmonics are an extension of the cluster process
in *De natura sonoris* No. 2. Penderecki's instruction for players to choose
their own 'highest fourth-flageolet' (i.e. artificial harmonic) creates the
cluster automatically.

Sciarrino takes a further step in *Da un divertimento* for ensemble. He
requires the strings to use a metal and a leather (or plastic) mute. Also
the tail-piece 'must be made of wood and not of plastic material'. The
notation is complex in appearance and sound, but the requirements
are thoroughly explained with no particular innovations involved. For
the conductor there is good news in that the pulse is always regular
in each movement. This is also the case in Ligeti's *Atmosphères*. But
the beating has to be done in such a way that any suggestion of pulse
in the performance must be avoided. Ligeti is so sensitive about the
implications of the title that the score contains a detailed preface
including a heading 'Remarks concerning rehearsal'. The instructions
emphasise the importance of ultra-quiet articulation in the woodwind
and brass together with a manner of bowing in the strings which avoids
any kind of accentuation. Each section of the work must 'melt' into the
other most of the time at a dynamic level of *pppp*. What appears in the
score to be complex rhythmic counterpoint should, in performance, be a
misty flow of constantly changing textures in which no single instrument
obtrudes. In rehearsal the conductor must make this an absolute priority
in formulating a manner of bowing and wind articulation explained
by Ligeti as 'played imperceptibly and *dolcissimo*'. Beating time at the
unchanging tempo of ♩ = 40 will not in itself achieve this beautiful
quality of sound images required. Such imperceptible articulation is
reminiscent of Furtwängler's manner in his final recording of *Tristan
und Isolde*. In the Prelude he achieved a *molto sostenuto* of such beauty

EXAMPLE 31 György Ligeti, *Atmosphères*

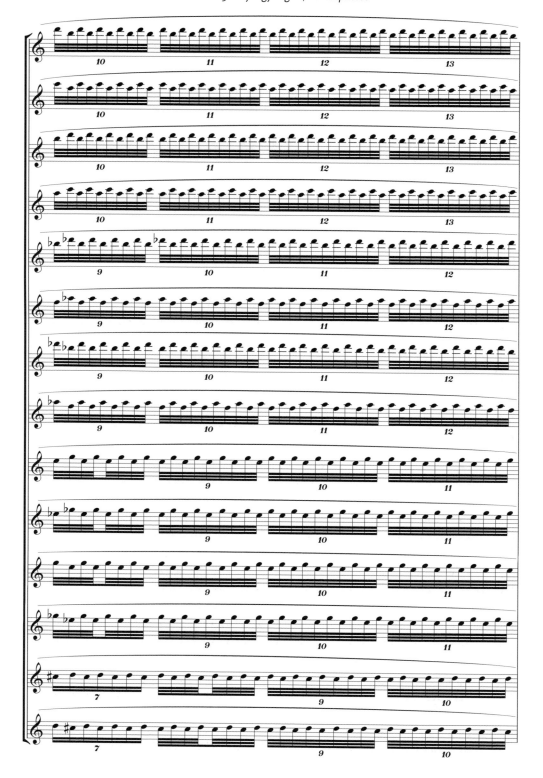

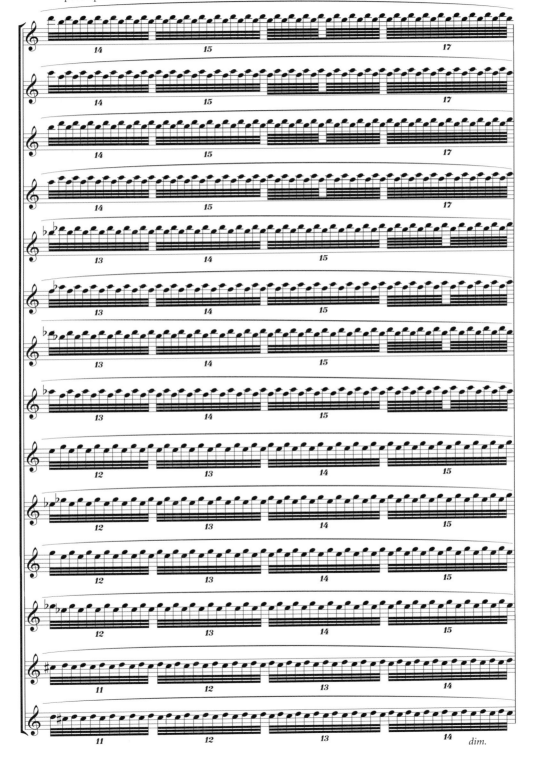

that it seems that each bow is a mile long. Although eccentric, the gently wavering beat which he uses is aimed at producing exactly the velvet quality of articulation which Ligeti desires.

Unlike *Tristan und Isolde*, *Atmosphères* sometimes contains explicit rhythmic unison in the multiple subdivisions within the same unit in the divided strings. The manner of beating must achieve the intensely sustained *pianissimo* but at the same time keeping the rhythmic unison intact at a very slow tempo. The solution I offer is to practise the manner with a metronome set at 40. Each beat should begin from the base-line in arch shapes which rise as high as the nose. Subdividing the slow pulse counting up to 6 the arm should rise very slowly, getting slower towards the top, then fall only on reaching number 6 in the counting. The fall should be gentle and much faster than the rise, caressing the base-line, but rising again immediately. It is the 'bouncing ball' principle taken to an extreme, again underlining the sense of anticipation which the players need for exact correlation of the unaccented pulse moments, but sustaining their independent subdivisions within the unit.

Example 31 shows one unit of a section with fifty-six subdivided strings. It begins as long sustained two-note oscillations which gradually develop into what is essentially a rapid *tremolando*. In rehearsal it is helpful for the players to practise with a subdivided beat. This might seem irrational when the number of notes in a unit is irrational, but it is essential that the ultimate variety of unit figurations, especially the slower ones, in the lower register, are distinguishable in the texture. Once an approximation has been achieved with a subdivided beat, the slow crotchet beat will establish an understanding for the players of all the related oscillations within the ensemble. When the pulse is reduced to $\lrcorner$ = 30 at H the prescription for beating at the previous tempo is even more important. In practising the manner of such a slow pulse it is helpful to mentally subdivide the beat (as in $\lrcorner$ = 40) by eight, but begin to fall on the seventh count. The minim pulse is essential because of the irrational subdivisions of 3 and 5 in many of the parts.

A glance at the score of Thomas Tallis's forty-part motet, *Spem in alium*, will make some of the pages in *Atmosphères* look familiar, but with even more parts, none of which contain the same linear formation of pitches and very few values, as in the Tallis. Both are works of intense

beauty and imagination. To realise the fragile delicacy of Ligeti's work
a great deal of rehearsal time is needed for its nineteen pages of score.
Beating a very slow tempo is more difficult than might be imagined. This
is evident in some recordings and performances of Sibelius's Symphony
no. 7 in which the beginning and end of the work have the same tempo,
approximating to ♩ = 44 (almost the minim equivalent of the crotchet
in *Atmosphères*). While the work begins with crotchet movement at 88
the string episode following the opening is in a minim format. It has to
be conducted in minims to achieve the intense and beautiful *sostenuto*
required:

EXAMPLE 32 Jean Sibelius, Symphony no. 7

This section can be spoiled by any increase in the tempo when a
conductor fails to control the excessively slow pulse. The close of the work
is also dependent on this tempo and can be too abrupt if the original
Adagio is not sustained. In spite of the 3/2 pulse indicated at the opening

it is important to note that Sibelius puts a crotchet in brackets after the *Adagio* indication; i.e. = 88 in my suggested tempo.

In relating aspects of the works discussed with music of other eras my intention is to underline aesthetic parallels which exist. Theoretic dogmatism can distort the understanding of any kind of music. This applies as much to composers as to performers. *Musica ficta* in the Renaissance opened the way to the chromatic functions of diatonic harmony in the Baroque era. Such a connection does not change the aesthetic response we have to either language or indeed to the motivations of the composers of either age. When performing modern works with students I have often found it necessary to encourage them to play, say, Lutosławski as if they were playing Wagner and to assert their own subjective artistry in the expression of the music. I consider such connections to be a vital ingredient in performing any music. This is equally important when electronics enter the repertoire.

□ □ □ □

From 1950 electronic music developed on its own path with the complex and time-consuming process of analogue technology. In 1956 the first real masterpiece arrived in the form of Stockhausen's *Gesang der Jünglinge*. With the composition of his *Mixtur* in 1964 the path was established for the development of works which combined electronics with orchestral instruments in performance. Stockhausen explains: 'In this way it becomes possible to obtain in conjunction with the use of instruments a differentiated composition of timbres such I had hitherto only been able to achieve in the realm of electronic music.' This is the point in the evolution of electronic music when the conductor enters the arena. With the arrival of digital technology later in the century the new resources were deployed in a vast range of possibilities and with much greater facility in the composition process, making the conductor's role more and more challenging.

There are two main categories for music which combine orchestral instruments or voices with electronics. If the electronic element involves prerecorded audio on any analogue or digital support without treatments on live instruments the works are categorised as *With Tape*. When electronic devices such as computers, keyboards, synthesizers or samplers are combined with instruments or voices on stage the works are categorised as using *Live Electronics*. The nature of this relationship between a computer and live instruments has also created the term 'interactive'. There is no absolute necessity to have expertise in the technology involved in order to conduct music which involves combining orchestral instruments or voices with electronics. But such works demand that the aural perception of the conductor can fully comprehend what is implicit in the electronic element of the music, especially when the sound sources are complex.

Orchestra/ensemble with tape or multi-channel computer-processed sound

In works which involve prerecorded sound to be played concurrently with live orchestral instruments or voices, the conductor has to identify the sounds on the tape in the course of rehearsal and performance. Some scores provide basic graphics which symbolise the tape part while others simply identify numbered cues for each tape entry. In either case it is imperative that the prerecorded tape be learned thoroughly by the conductor. Only with this preparation can the co-ordination of prerecorded tape and live instruments be achieved. This process is represented in several scores by Jonathan Harvey. His *Inner Light 1* demonstrates a remarkable sensitivity and imaginative blending of both elements. The composer has included a graphic representation of the prerecorded tape which includes specific cues for the conductor to identify.

EXAMPLE 33 Jonathan Harvey, *Inner Light 1*

When the notation for the instruments is free or spatial, as in Example 33, an aspect of learning the tape part relates to determining the events as they are introduced by counting in seconds. In marking up my own score as it appears in Example 33, at the bottom of the page I have specified the duration in seconds between each cue on the tape. Above this, in brackets, I have marked the instrumental cues (also in seconds) in a secondary system for signalling the instrumental entries. This is a safeguard which accommodates the very quiet entry of each sound on the tape. It is essential that each tape entry should complement the live instrument. Simply learning the tape sounds without a breakdown in seconds can create poor co-ordination.

As in many such works the tape does not function in instrumental episodes. The electronics performer will stop running the tape and restart at a subsequent section. It is very important that the conductor cues each new entry for the electronics performer with a left-hand signal. Raising the left hand high at least two bars before the cue provides an assured re-entry of the tape. As each entry has a track number, it is not a problem for the electronics musician to start at any point in rehearsal if a bar number is specified by the conductor.

Roger Reynolds has extended the relationship of prerecorded tape to accompany a live performance in a work which transforms the recorded sound of instrumental music using multiphonics in the process. In his *Transfigured Wind II* he used the computer as a vital element in the transformation of natural recorded sound. After composing a piece for solo flute and recording it as a complete performance he used it as a sound source for transformations, which involved the subjective input of the soloist. Reynolds explains that 'Once inside the computer [the recorded performance] underwent a host of transformations before re-emerging on the tape.' The score is very explicit in the relationship between the flute soloist, the orchestra and the tape. The conductor's role, especially in rehearsal, is to achieve the integration and balancing of these three elements, in which the material is designed to convey anticipation, reflection and recall. The computer treatments of the flute solo act as a transforming reflection of the live flute solo in the performance. Such an imaginative perception requires an equally imaginative approach from the conductor to achieve what the composer

84

Orchestra/ensemble with
tape or multi-channel
computer-processed sound

describes as 'otherworldly reflections of and upon the soloist's specifics'. With this in mind, the technical issues for performance relate to rehearsal strategy.

Initial rehearsal will only involve instrumentalists. As all sections of the work are crotchet-orientated there are no beating issues for the conductor to deal with. In the opening section Reynolds requests woodwinds to use 'overblowing and/or special fingerings'. As with many other composers he does not specify multiphonic fingerings, leaving it to the players to produce a strong articulation for a chord or a lightened embouchure and lots of breath support for overblowing on the flute. For players who are not familiar with these techniques it is recommended that the reed instrumentalists use what is called 'double-fork fingering', that is, closing finger-plates 1 and 3 with both hands, leaving each middle finger open. This is a chord that is easily produced, but will give a differing harmonic spectrum on each instrument.

With tape restarts for each number Reynolds has made it possible to rehearse each section as many times as necessary without creating problems for such repeated restarts.

When combining all three elements in rehearsal Reynolds has arranged the tape part in a similar manner to Harvey's *Inner Light 1* so that the individual sections can be stopped and restarted.

Example 34 also indicates the importance of a preparatory left-hand signal for the electronics performer before cueing the tape entry. Although not specified, the composer's instructions to the conductor indicate the need to separate the function of each hand – the right to cue each string entry in bar 1, the left to cue the tape entry.

This score is full of subtle, expressive gestures for the instrumentalists, but the notes on the page cannot convey all that is required from performers. The conductor has to monitor such detail in judging the balance and interrelated responses required by the three individual elements. Learning the tape by itself before considering the instrumental parts is a safe way to digest the imaginative ingredients of the work and to understand the intense relationship between each element.

The co-ordination of prepared tape and live instruments gives the conductor a different kind of challenge in Stockhausen's *Trans*. A large platform is required to accommodate the visual element and the complex

EXAMPLE 34 Roger Reynolds, *Transfigured Wind II*

sound distribution involved in the work. At the front of the platform forty string players are arranged in two rows, the rear one on a raised platform. Behind them four separate groups of wind, brass and percussion players are arranged in a semicircle formation, numbered I–IV in the score. The conductor sits in the middle, behind the strings, concealed by a black screen. It is essential that the four groups and conductor are not seen by the audience. Each group is amplified by individual loudspeakers. This is also the case for three soloists: trumpet (who ascends a high platform for a solo), viola and cello. An electric organ is also involved with a separate loudspeaker. The strings are illuminated by a violet-red, misty light. This is a brief explanation of the staging instructions which are extended and elaborated in the score.

Accompanying this is a prerecorded stereo tape which produces periodic articulations of a weaving-loom sound. These sounds are reproduced over two loud- speakers to the left and right of the strings. The string players sustain very long single notes in a hypnotic manner, only changing to different notes at each projection of the weaving-loom sound, which is moderately explosive. Governed by a wide-ranging number of differing metronome marks in the score the conductor has to be absolutely exact in the varying tempi in order to meet the loom articulations at exactly the right moment of co-ordination each time. Any miscalculation will create disaster. As there are forty-seven changes of metronome marks in the piece, the conductor's mental metronome has to be utterly reliable. This is a fundamental requirement for all musicians, but it is especially important for a conductor dealing with this kind of repertoire. It is easy to become complacent and over-confident in one's ability to judge tempi correctly. In conventional music the tempo does not necessarily have to be defined in metronomic terms, but no matter how thoroughly digested Stockhausen's score might be the varying tempi are not so easily judged and maintained in performance. Because this is the main technical attribute here it is not an elementary exercise for a conductor to make constant tests of tempi perceptions with a metronome while learning the score. In performance there can be an inclination to push the tempo in anticipation of the loom articulation out of concern not to be too late. This psychological impulse must always be resisted. It should be kept in mind that we are not pulse machines and that during a prolonged period in a constant tempo we will create minute divergences. In this piece it is comforting to know that the release noise of the shuttle sound is anticipated by a 'shshsh' sound before the explosion is released. This provides room for slight adjustment of the beat if necessary – a situation which it is wise to explain to the orchestra in rehearsal. All aspects of beat formation discussed previously will contribute to the economical use of rehearsal time and the security of co-ordination in performance.

It is unusual to find the word 'authenticity' occurring in a discussion of modern music. In the case of Stockhausen it is an important issue. Most of the composer's music involving electronics and tape was composed in the days of analogue technology. It was the composer's wish that all of these works should be performed with the original technology involved. While digital technology has its own merits, on the issue of the quality of sound production, the original vinyl recording of *Gesang der Jünglinge* (1958) is arguably unbeatable. In relation to works with tape the 'authentic' agenda could result in ultimate obsolescence.

□ □ □ □

Click-track involvement

In scores which combine continuous prerecorded tape with live instruments, a click-track is often required to sustain the vertical cohesion between the two elements. This is usually an integral specification for the conductor, who will need to practise the pulse requirements with the tape before rehearsing as part of the score preparation. Beating time to a click-track which sustains the same pulse and time-signature throughout does not require comment. When tempi and irregular pulse are variable the conductor's role becomes quite challenging and complex. Such a work is Tristan Murail's *Désintégrations* ('pour bande synthétisée et 17 instruments'). Because the complete work is based on crotchet units with occasional fractional additions, time-signatures are replaced by integers, not only for convenience but also to relate to the click-track graphics, which are placed between bars as dotted lines.

This is especially useful when a subdivision of the unit has to be beaten, as in the sixth bar of Example 35. During pause bars when the ensemble is silent, the click is not present. In these bars Murail provides three cue clicks before the next ensemble entry, which are included in the score as in the opening bar of Example 35. With earphones in place the conductor has to combine listening intensely to the click-track while focusing equally on the instrumental ensemble. 'Open earphones' of the 'Walkman' type are recommended by the composer. As the sounds on the tape are derived from instrument sources, there is a close integration of the live and prerecorded elements which must always be balanced by the conductor in association with the electronics performer. The composer states that 'there is one origin for both tape and instruments, their relationship being one of complementarity. The title of the piece refers to how the tape element 'diffracts or disintegrates their [the instruments'] timbre'. So there are three elements which the conductor has to relate to: the tape, the click-track and the live ensemble. The earphones are the most important part of the control required. An alternative to the kind of earphones the composer recommends are open headphones, often used in recording studios. Place the headpiece in such a position that only one ear is covered by an earphone, keeping the other available for live hearing.

EXAMPLE 35 Tristan Murail, *Désintégrations*

EXAMPLE 36 Tristan Murail, *Désintégrations*

In this way balance can be established easily and adjustment of the headpiece unnecessary in rehearsal discussion. An even better alternative is provided by single-ear headphones.

As in the Harvey work, in rehearsal it is possible to cut in at various places in the score where convenient for the electronics performer. Murail's score has its eleven cues marked in Roman numerals, equivalent to the tracks. Because they relate to possible cut-in places on the tape it is sometimes considered unnecessary to have bar numbers marked in the score. If a score lacks bar numbers, as in this case, it saves time in instrumental rehearsals to add them to the score and parts.

When Murail's click-track relates to even crotchets and simple subdivisions, conducting is mostly a matter of clear time-beating and cueing. At the section in Example 36 matters become more complicated.

The composer's explanation of time units indicates that the third bar will become compound units. Because there is also an accelerando involved, plus the metronome mark changes from the initial ♩ = 75, the written units I have added at the top of the third bar might be a useful preparatory calculation for practising the very divergent pulses on the click-track. I have also enlarged additional indications of the metronome marks for clear reference. While there is the blessing of a pause bar over the page there is no excuse for damaging the clarity of the rhythmic unison required in the instrumental ensemble. Asserting the beating manner of Stravinsky's 'Glorification de l'élue' (p. 24) is an essential ingredient in the control required.

I can think of a number of works in which graphic mistakes have escaped an editor in a publication. *Désintégrations* is no exception. In case the reader wishes to prepare the score for performance it is useful to know that while practising the pacing with the tape, at two bars before number VII two beats to a bar are indicated whereas the click-track subdivides into four for four bars, and back into two at the third bar of VII. The same thing happens in the last bar of p. 63 for four bars and between bars 339 and 349 in which the click-track beats in quavers until returning to crotchets in bar 349. The rather eccentric indications of time units practised in some scores of Messiaen, while perfectly logical, can be disconcerting. In *Désintégrations* 3/2 does not mean three minims! Because of the incessant changes of pulse throughout this section I have written it out in conventional time-signatures. None of the click-track pulses is the same from one beat to another in the section containing my amendments placed below the original.

EXAMPLE 37 Tristan Murail, *Désintégrations*:
the graphics of electronic music involving click-tracks

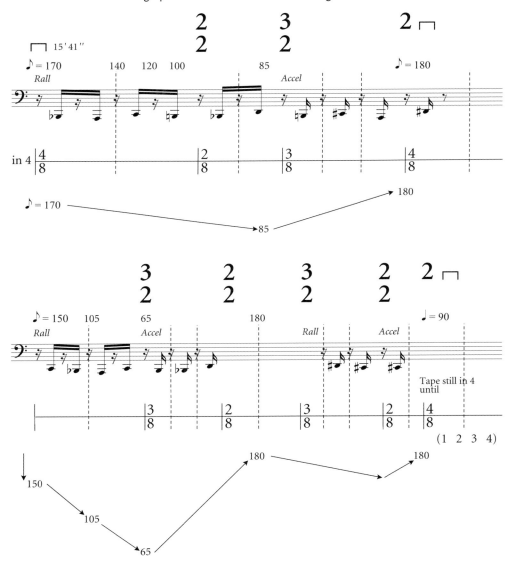

Désintégrations is a complex score to learn, but the piece is very exciting in its application of the spectral theories which Murail and Gérard Grisey established in the 1980s.

□ □ □ □

The repertoire in which instruments or voices are electronically treated in live performance are mostly of a solo or small ensemble nature. Jonathan Harvey's *From Silence* for soprano, six instruments and live electronics has the voice treated with a harmoniser, which transposes the vocal production to several parallel intervals. Cristóbal Halffter's *Planto por las víctimas de la violencia* uses live electronic transformations of several instruments. It is a process less used in the symphony orchestra because any instrument which is treated requires the use of a microphone. Any other instrument close to the one being treated will also be picked up by the microphone. My own work for large orchestra, *Saturn*, solves the issue with the inclusion of four soloists set apart from the main orchestra. There are episodes in the work when instruments in the main body of the orchestra are electronically treated. When these sections are completed the related microphones are switched off. Initially, the solo group plays with the full orchestra, but treated by a tape delay system which introduces what has been recorded at a later stage, signalled by the conductor. At the first episode in the work, delays are superimposed on the live performance, requiring exact metronomic alignment with live and recorded playback. For this to work the conductor has to use a 'silent' metronome with a flashing light so that a constant tempo of $\quarternote = 100$ is sustained to combine both elements of the score with pulse unison.

The work is a celebration of the arrival of Voyager II at Saturn in 1980 with the discovery that the planet had many more satellites than were previously known. With Holst's 'Saturn chord' as the organism for the work, it is a homage to the great composer. The names of the major satellites function as motivations for free variations. 'Tethys' involves woodwind multiphonics with specific fingerings to produce the pitches of the written chords exactly, but with the added dimension of ring modulation treatment, which transforms the chords with a wide range of added harmonics (Example 38).

The planet is dark and black, inviting the otherwordly character of the resulting music. While the fingerings for the multiphonics are explicit in producing the required pitches in the untreated chord, the ring modulation adds harmonics which are of uncertain origin. It is not

EXAMPLE 38 Edwin Roxburgh, *Saturn*, 'Tethys'

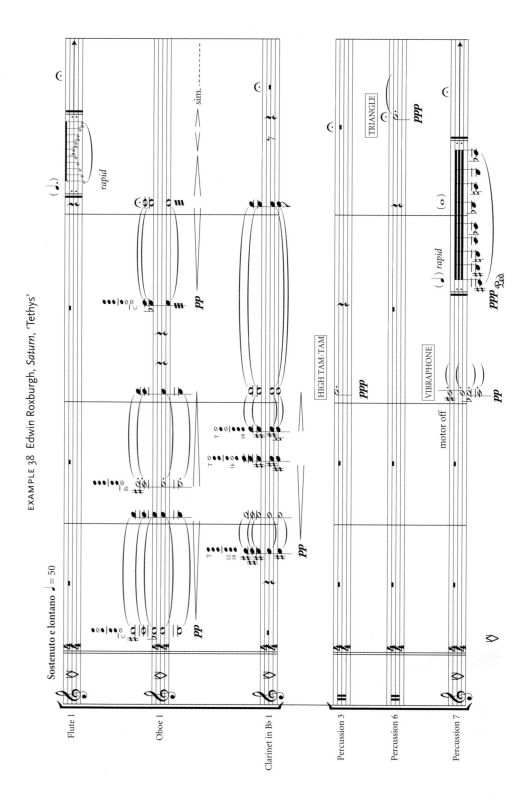

possible for the conductor to imagine the pitches and sound involved. With such an issue it is essential to test the correct pitches produced by the players in rehearsal prior to electronic involvement. The fingering for the instruments will work on any mechanism system. If the pitches are correct the treatments will produce the desired result. The function of the delay system in other sections of the work is cued by the conductor as instructed in the score.

When a composer combines multiphonics and electronic elements with a large orchestra the conductor's responsibilities go well beyond the normal requirements in that the balance of each element has to be a constant consideration while in rehearsal. Also, the live electronic element cannot be assessed adequately until the orchestra is present. Add to this the graphic complexity which requires equally complex directing techniques and the conductor's task becomes very different from the role required for standard repertoire. In confronting such a score we should be constantly concerned about the aesthetic of the music and its artistic content.

One of the most complex scores in this category is Boulez's *Répons*. Using the state-of-the-art resources at IRCAM in the early 1980s, Boulez was able to construct the work with a vast array of electronic equipment, including thirty-eight loudspeakers, eight stereo equalisers for diffusion and twenty-four audio lines for linking the six soloists to the mixers. This was one of the first works to use digital technology to treat solo instruments in live performance. Apart from the six soloists there is a chamber ensemble together with computer-generated sound. Transformation of the sounds of the soloists involves delay, frequency-shifting and modulation, transmitted by microphones to a digital-signal processor and then to the speakers.

While there are no improvised elements in the work there are many sections which contain independent performance of individual instruments against an element which is rhythmically controlled by the conductor. The latter often include multiple grace-note flourishes indicated by a time unit integer with a cross through it. The score is in manuscript. Although it is large and complex the fundamental techniques for conducting it are explained in relation to *Le Marteau sans mâitre* in Part Three.

The spatial layout of the performers recommended in the score is problematic for most performance venues because the orchestra has to be set up in the centre of an auditorium with the audience arranged in a circle around the performers. By 1995 the ideal concert hall was built in Paris. The Cité de la Musique has a raised balcony for the audience which surrounds the performing arena below. It is a perfect arena for this and other works which involve the spatial projection of electronic elements.

Many of the works in this category are not complex in relation to the technique required of a conductor. The challenge arises in balancing several electronic elements with live instrumentalists. York Höller's *Pensées* demonstrates an immensely sensitive sound-world created by disparate sound sources. A large symphony orchestra is combined with a solo pianist playing a MIDI grand piano, which controls computer-generated sounds and digital filters, together with a quadraphonic tape which produces only electronic sounds. The conductor's task is to achieve in rehearsal the fusion of these elements to the point where it is sometimes impossible to distinguish electronic from orchestral sound. Practical considerations are first on the list when arranging a performance. It is extremely important for the conductor to have at least two rehearsals with the pianist at the MIDI grand piano. As this has to be hired for a period within budget restraints it is a critical consideration in the rehearsal arrangements, especially as the instrument requires proper setting up by an electronics performer. The soloist will also need practice time on the unfamiliar instrument. Once in place it is the conductor's task to learn and digest the wide variety of tone colours contained in the solo part. After this preparation rehearsals can be pursued with a concept of the interrelationship between all the elements of the score.

The presence of Bach/Berg references in many parts of the music indicates a reverential character of contemplation which is occasionally interrupted by passionate outbursts with full orchestra. The four-track tape enters following the unconducted cadenza involving MIDI piano and synthesizer. Co-ordinating the tape part (which should be thoroughly learned) with the orchestra can be done, as in *Trans*, without a click-track. But for absolute co-ordination the use of a mechanical form of pulse at 60 is a wise precaution. A final recommendation is to provide a strong cue for the pianist at Figure 39 in the score.

Jonathan Harvey, like Reynolds, is reputedly one of the finest composers in this category. *Valley of Aosta* is a pinnacle of his achievement in merging live with electronic sound sources. Two DX7 II synthesizers are employed, one of which is tuned a quarter-tone sharp. One keyboard is placed above the other for a single performer. Speaker levels are controlled from a mixing desk in the auditorium. A computer is also employed for three sequences specified in the score as MIDI Sequences 1, 2 and 3. It is important for the conductor to cue each of these entries. This is also essential at bar 256 where the keyboard enters after a long silence. Example 39 shows the entry of the third sequence.

From here, a long and gradual accelerando is specified over thirteen bars. It is helpful to the players if bars similar to 210 in this section are subdivided. This will also assist in controlling the accelerando to almost double the speed by bar 222 – at which point the pianist needs a cue.

Like Reynolds, Harvey underlines the importance of balance. This is very specific in Harvey's instruction for the 2nd synthesizer in Example 39. Texture is closely associated with this, as explained in the composer's instruction: 'the ensemble uses related colours which shift frequently: sax relates to tpt. in its high register, cor-anglais in its low register: two harps (tuned a quarter-tone apart) relate to two synthesizers (also tuned a quarter-tone apart) in their 'plucked' timbres, and so on.'

Example 39 illustrates a characteristic which is a hallmark of Harvey's polyphony. Bar 209 shows totally independent motivic substance in each instrument. The result is a glistening texture constantly changing throughout the section. For the conductor to be 'the composer's advocate'[8] in such a work, every note of every instrument, including the synthesizers, must be thoroughly learned. In rehearsal it is essential to be aware of every note and nuance in the score. As with all complex works, dissection of the score in sectional rehearsal is the only way to secure detailed preparation of the performance in the interest of the composer and the performers. This also provides each instrumentalist with the means to project their parts with the soloistic approach required (even in *pp*) to realise the complex texture the composer has created.

The technology associated with this and other works involving electronics is a constantly evolving medium. Synthesizers are especially prone to obsolescence. Harvey gives an appropriate warning in his

EXAMPLE 39 Jonathan Harvey, *Valley of Aosta*

score: 'updatings of these technical arrangements will be made in the future as necessary'. Some of the works discussed were created on analogue systems, many of which have now been transferred to digital. Having many of the programmes available on line makes performance preparation a much more convenient process. For the conductor this means that rehearsal time can be used without delays, as long as the electronic involvements are studied carefully with the assistance of an electronics performer. Current technology will always be an aspect of enquiry in scheduling rehearsals and performances. This extra dimension in a conductor's world is an important ingredient in the evolution of the language of music. The conductor is part of that process.

With the twenty-first century the computer becomes a more subtle agent in the treatment of instruments in live performance. In Lamberto Coccioli's *Aluna,* for viola, ensemble and live electronics, it is used to transform the sound of the orchestra by using a viola – its pitch, amplitude and spectral content – as both a generator and a controller of the electronic treatments. The result is a colourful and dramatic array of interactions which culminate in the viola becoming isolated from the ensemble, sustaining an intense high note with the live electronic treatments carrying it to the close.

The initial rehearsal is the first time the conductor is able to hear the complete effect of the score. Unlike the Harvey works discussed it is impossible for the composer to include any graphics for the electronic involvement beyond the cues which indicate when electronic events are triggered. As with other works in this category, reserving the left hand to direct each of the thirty-six cues is advisable. While the conducting gestures required are conventional, the incisive rhythmic counterpoint serves a rich, textural palette, in which the details of phrasing, articulation and dynamic variants must inform the performance and the conductor's perception, if the electronic involvement is to be effective. Without such precision the performance will fail. It is an ideal work to illustrate the equality of interaction and integration of electronics with live instruments in the performance arena. The evolution of the language of music will intensify this relationship. The conductor's need to comprehend its implications in score preparation is an imperative element in his/her responsibilities.

At the time of writing, electronics is a specialised element of training in conservatoires and university departments, mainly for composers. As the medium will become more and more integrated with music for instruments and voices, this evolutionary process will require electronics to be a foundation aspect of music education for all music students. This is especially important for conductors, because composers are progressively including more and more graphic information in scores which include electronic elements. The Reynolds score (p. 85) is an example of this development. In learning and preparing a new work with electronics, the conductor should have an equally informed understanding of this part of the score as the instrumental and vocal. This will create a good foundation for collaboration with the electronics performer and give the conductor the essential control of all aspects of the score in a performance.

☐ ☐ ☐ ☐

Most of the repertoire of choral music composed since 1950 does not call for the use of conducting techniques relating to this book. It is much more difficult for singers to pitch notes in a chromatically based work than it is for an instrumentalist, whose displacement of fingers automatically produces correct pitches. Most composers demonstrate an awareness of this in avoiding complex pulses and variable time-units. However, there are some vocal works which do require exceptional rehearsal procedures which do not fall within the normal specialist field of choral conductors. Irrational note-groups and their subdivisions within a unit exact tremendous concentration from singers. Such a work is Ligeti's *Lux aeterna* for sixteen-part mixed *a cappella* choir. The following recommendations might be considered by choral and instrumental conductors.

Example 40 shows Ligeti in his familiar crotchet-orientated graphics. None of the sixteen voices articulate their notes at exactly the same time. Unless the displacements are exact the effect of the music will fail. The whole piece is very quiet and calm. Ligeti requests all the voices in the choir to sing totally without accents: 'bar lines have no rhythmic significance and should not be emphasized'. It is not easy for singers to enter in a subdivided unit on, for instance, the third quintuplet subdivision of a crotchet without making an emphatic articulation. The technique for unaccented articulations must be developed in rehearsal by the person who is to conduct the performance.

There are three issues of technique to be considered:

1 The intonation of chromatic intervals in the four parts which are not related to diatonic harmony.

2 Unaccentuated articulations in a sustained line.

3 Sustaining a consistent *pp* dynamic in long phrases.

EXAMPLE 40 György Ligeti, *Lux aeterna*

Example 41 is offered as a preparatory exercise, which involve these three characteristics. At first it is helpful if each of the items is practised individually so that aural perception can be formed and established in a concentrated way. As always, repetition will create a habit which can gradually become automatic in application. By practising the chromatic scales in each voice, the non-diatonic relationships in the chords will become familiar territory in the aural reception of the singers. The perfect 5th in the last chord will act as a determinant for intonation. Before adding the words to the exercise the unaccented articulations may be as a moving *legato* line on one syllable, to achieve the smooth elision needed when all the syllables are added. All of these exercises will help to achieve the ultimate goal if they are rehearsed at a *pp* dynamic.

EXAMPLE 41 Preparatory vocal exercise for György Ligeti, *Lux aeterna*

Choral conductors might agree that analogies can sometimes be helpful in achieving a common understanding of the character of a work. To avoid any accentuation of the syllables think of the image of a light bulb going on or fingers opening from a fist position rather than the percussive attack of a side drum. I am aware that performance instructions do not always involve explanations of the technique required of the performer. While Ligeti is explicit and clear in performance instructions, the way in which they are applied requires a subtle expertise from a conductor if the result is to avoid a mechanical presentation.

Applying such a preparation for *Lux aeterna*, emphasis must be placed on the entry of each calculation being at eleven different points in the subdivisions of the crotchet unit. I have numbered them in Example 26. These subdivisions are consistent in each voice, but sometimes the point of displacement varies. So, for instance, in B2 the quintuplet-related entries are made at different points in the subdivided unit. This needs rhythmic practice, as in all the other parts. Sectional rehearsal with those in quintuplets, then triplets and finally semiquaver subdivisions will help to achieve the rhythmic independence of each voice. As with rhythmic structures in instrumental music it is helpful if, at first, the singers avoid listening to each other and simply concentrate on their individual parts. This would be bad advice in performing Mozart, but the essence of this piece is dependent on the exact displacement of all entries. Once mastered, the result is exquisitely beautiful.

There are many examples in the choral repertoire where such polyphony is completely absent. Except for a short episode Gabriel Jackson's *Ave, Regina caelorum* sustains rhythmic unison in all of the voices in a powerful paean of joy. Against the Latin text in the choir a solo soprano sings a Christina Rossetti poem, the last section accompanied by a free *ad lib. parlando* from the choir. The conductor's art must be applied to balancing the solo electric guitar, which pursues an active commentary against the choir and soloist with an instruction at one point to play 'like Eric Clapton'. It is a distinctive idea which can generate a strongly projected performance from the singers, who are not (like the guitar) amplified. It is a conductor's responsibility to check and advise on the placement of speakers to achieve the sense of balance in the dialogue between the voices and the guitar.

The electric guitar is also used by Luciano Berio in a work which involves a singer in a provocative context. His collaboration with Edoardo Sanguineti in *Passaggio* resulted in a work involving two choruses (one displaced around the audience), a soprano soloist and a large chamber ensemble involving five percussionists. The conductor has to control all four elements at the same time. There is an ensemble for woodwind, brass, percussion and strings. One of the two choruses has spoken roles and is seated widely around the auditorium, amongst the audience. The other is a singing chorus on stage. A solo soprano is required to perform voluptuous acting together with a challenging vocal part. It is doubtful if amateur singers could meet the pitching demands of the on-stage chorus, but professional singers have the experience to focus on the un-cued pitches which the work requires. It is essential to arrange a rehearsal schedule which caters for at least one sectional rehearsal for each element alone. Where spatial notation is involved, the conducting requirements are similar to Boulez's *Pli selon pli* (discussed on pp. 45–51). Applied here the conducting signals are less complicated, but require consistency of timing and pacing in each rehearsal. The work does not involve technical explanation beyond what has already been examined in other works.

While it is tempting to develop a discussion of vocal music by introducing opera it would be inappropriate for the purposes of this book. Even when performers read from scores in performance it is challenging for a choir to sing works with a chromatic language involved. When the vocal parts in a work lasting three hours or more have to be memorised and acted it would be arrogant of any composer to deploy complex rhythmic and intricate motivic material. Composing for the voice is a very different art from composing for instruments. This is reflected in the lucid and fluent writing in Benjamin Britten's operas, which adhere to diatonic material for the voices most of the time. While issues of register arise in Thomas Adès's *A Midsummer Night's Dream* there are no complex pulses involved for the singers. Ligeti's *Le Grand Macabre* depends almost entirely on a crotchet unit and conventional time-signatures throughout. Stockhausen finds an intriguing solution in the second act of his *Donnerstag*, from the opera-cycle *Licht*, by introducing instrumentalists on stage as characters in the plot. Such extremes are avoided by Mark-Anthony Turnage where rhythmic characteristics are distilled from jazz. In all cases the conductor relies entirely on a conventional technique in which clarity of gesture and an ability to take on *répétiteur* responsibilities in the rehearsal process is paramount. Beyond this a separate book is needed.

□ □ □ □

PART TWO
Other voices

So far, the broad principles of conducting the music being considered
have constituted the recommendations of one musician – the author. He
will readily admit that the techniques he recommends are by no means
the only workable guide. There are so many issues related to successful
conducting which cannot be explained, especially in relation to the
character and personality of individual conductors. The most important
criteria come from those who actually play or sing the music, whose
performing is either inspired or frustrated by a conductor. For this reason
I consider it of vital importance to address their views in examining the
relationship between the conductor and those he/she directs. I have also
sought the views of other conductors and composers in addressing the
issues of performance. The quotations from Leon Botstein, Lamberto
Coccioli, Lionel Friend, David Hockings, Nona Lidell, Jane Manning,
Anthony Payne, Julian Pike, Ross Pople, David Purser, Nicholas Reed, Joel
Sachs, Timothy Salter and David Wordsworth are drawn from interviews
I had with them. All the musicians quoted have wide experience of
performing and dealing with the challenging repertoire under discussion.

□ □ □ □

The methodology proposed in Part One underlines basic principles rather than rules. Boulez's caveat confronts the issue directly: 'To imitate the gestures of other conductors is completely useless, since it's a question of length of arm, suppleness of hands, technique with or without a baton, of physiognomy even.'[1] During their professional lives instrumentalists are directed by a vast number of different conductors, all of whom are distinctive in their techniques and artistry. Their preferences and requirements can be the substance of heated debate in the band room, both positive and negative. But there is considerable agreement on the qualities which make it possible for them to produce an impressive performance, both for the audience and themselves. 'Clarity of gesture' is the common call. Nona Liddell recalls her experience with conductors when she was principal violin in the London Sinfonietta. While she acknowledges the clarity, intelligence and assurance of some, it is knowledge of the score which impresses her most. In complex scores it is easy for a conductor to be overwhelmed by the technical issues involved at the expense of the aesthetic characteristics of the music. It is this which concerns her when a conductor fails to 'internalise' a performance, so that the gestures become mechanical. When the geometry of the beat is complex there is a danger that exaggeration will obscure the musical endeavour with the perfectly good intention of providing clear direction for the players.

Also a member of the London Sinfonietta, the trombonist David Purser expresses concern when this failure of a conductor to 'internalise' (he uses the same word) affects pulse changes. He underlines the importance of expression in the gestural language, no matter how complicated the music becomes. The conductor must 'go beyond the beating process' is how he puts it. Ross Pople is a conductor who spent many years as principal cello in the BBC Symphony Orchestra and the London Sinfonietta before founding the London Festival Orchestra. He holds a similar view to that of Purser in stressing that 'time-beating has no meaning if heart and soul are absent' and that 'the conductor has failed if the players do not enjoy the music-making'. Purser gives an imaginative comment on a player's reaction to expressive conducting in relation to a performance of Harrison Birtwistle's *Silbury Air*: 'Following the conductor is less important than being able to play the music. It is inspiring when a conductor is able to give the sense of a magic trick going on in this kind of work.' In other words, the conductor's technique has to be married to the spirit and substance of the music – the projection of an internal perception which makes the external gestures look spontaneous and compelling to the players, even in a pulse piece like *Silbury Air*. Nona Liddell considers this work to be Birtwistle at his best. 'A brilliant idea which is not as difficult to play as it seems' is how she describes it. Such a comment from a performer is a gift to a composer and reassuring for a conductor. She also stresses that technique cannot be divorced from personality. 'Showing authority is to be welcomed, but not in a bullying way' is a view which informs her conclusions on the many conductors she has performed with in a wide range of composers. She identifies four conductors who project the essential qualities required for this repertoire. Rather than identifying them by name, I specify them as abstract numbers.

Conductor 1 'Excellent. Clear, assured and intelligent.'

Conductor 2 'Very musical, but not always secure. He pointed to himself if he made a mistake.' (She is more tolerant than the author in this regard!)

Conductor 3 'Excellent in clarity and knowledge of the score.'

Conductor 4 'Clear, but reserved. He never made eye-contact.'

She concludes that all of these conductors showed 'respect' for the players. 'Conductors who are abrupt and abrasive never get the best out of an orchestra. Creating confidence is essential.' Pople expresses a similar view to that of Liddell in relation to conductor 4. While admiring the intellectual rigour which informs his knowledge of the score, 'exacting rehearsal procedures never resulted in an inspired performance'.

The singer and author Jane Manning stresses the importance of the ingredient of personality, if a conductor is to achieve good results. 'Creating confidence is of prime importance' is a phrase of hers which is countered by an observation about conductor 4: 'Clear. But he doesn't involve you in performance and seems quite cold.' This emphasises the importance of technique being a mirror of personality, not an end in itself, even in judging a very distinguished musician. It is an adjunct of the essential relationship between gesture and concept as mutual attributes of technique. Leon Botstein is President of the Bard College and is a distinguished scholar and conductor. He supports this view by explaining that 'the conductor has to make an argument – to assert communicative logic in a performance'.

Jane Manning's view of conductor 4 is similar to that of Nona Liddell. They both retain admiration for his authority and clarity of gesture, but express concern about the absence of eye-contact and an apparent lack of involvement with the performers. Eye-contact is fundamental to the principles examined in Part One, but cannot be consistent from one work to another. A complex work might require excessive focus on every page of the score in performance. In which case the music stand should be in a position which allows the head to remain upwards to face the orchestra, so that only the eyes turn downwards towards to score. It is a quicker reflex for the eyes to move down and up rapidly than for the bowed head to perform the action. The extended arm and hand should always be within the same focus, no matter which section of the orchestra claims supportive attention. Eye-contact is high on the priorities of conducting any music, but especially in this repertoire.

In the classical and romantic repertoire an orchestra can play the music without a conductor quite effectively. The pianist/conductor, Joel Sachs, puts the point succinctly concerning much traditional music: 'If a conductor has no ideas he/she is unnecessary'. He continues: 'In much newer music, however, a conductor is required not only in order to focus an interpretation and to control the detail, pacing and balance in establishing an artistic performance, but also to secure a metric framework or, in some cases, co-ordinated improvisatory passages.' In the music under discussion there are further responsibilities and skills required. The range of percussion instruments available to composers has grown massively since 1950. As a result, the role of Head of Percussion in a symphony orchestra has become a complex and arduous preoccupation if the orchestra features contemporary music in its repertoire, such as the BBC Symphony and New York Philharmonic orchestras, especially when Boulez was their Director. The wide range of conductors which the percussionist David Hockings has experienced in heading the BBC Symphony Orchestra's percussion section gives him considerable authority on the issues a conductor should be aware of. His main points relate to practical issues.

When each percussionist is involved in playing in a station which occupies several different instruments, more than one music stand might be required. Moving from one instrument to another will involve taking eyes off the part *and* the conductor in order to relocate a playing position. Another consideration is that the percussion section is much further away from the rostrum than any other section of the orchestra. For these reasons Hockings states that 'the clarity of the down beat is an imperative'. As recommended on p. 15 this must be consistently in a central focus so that the eyes and the beat are seen in an undivided location. Whatever the character of the music, he recommends that the beat should be 'as large as possible' proportionate to the tempo. He underlines that consistency in the gesture is especially important in works with irregular pulse. On the issue of subdividing irregular beats he is equally firm: 'It can be too quick a gesture to be of value to the players in rapid tempi.' He adds that 'The conductor's task is to assist the players, not to control their playing of minute nuances within a pulse unit.' It is the author's view also that subdivision of the beat should be a last resort in any music. Players must be trusted to play motivic material between one unit and the next with their own musical integrity.

For a young percussionist (at the time of writing) who has inherited the legacy of music from 1950 into the twenty-first century, similar observations are made. Nicholas Reed (a fine soloist) emphasises the importance of 'an *innate*, highly sensitive sense of complex rhythm in a conductor, which has to serve expression as well'. He continues: 'Engaging the whole ensemble in the physical language used is the only interpretation of technique which percussion players can respond to.' The clarity of the central downbeat is again emphasised. He is in accord with Hockings in the 'give-and-take' relationship required between conductor and percussionists. Issues such as changing of mallets must be added to his list of considerations when 'a conductor decides to alter something in a rehearsal, such as a change of a previously set tempo'. Sometimes a conductor can overlook such important issues, being unaware that 'the percussion section might not be able to adapt to changes so spontaneously when physical alterations to a stick tray or a set-up have to be made'.

Practical issues in the relationship of players to conductors stretch beyond the distant percussionists. Boulez says that 'If the players are thirty metres away from the conductor one cannot ask them to look at their score and the conductor's beat at the same time.'[2] If this is so, how do players connect with the conductor's gestures in general? My own experience as an orchestral musician establishes that the player's eyes remain on the music most of the time, but *always* with the conductor in focus above the music stand, so that this dual connection is rarely absent. The conductor's awareness of this will emphasise the importance of clarity of gesture and eye-contact, especially in works which involve flexible metric structures.

In focusing on the conductor's responsibility to the players the composer and critic Anthony Payne extends the issue of the conductor's personality in the relationship. 'Authority is definitely needed, but it should be asserted in a way which facilitates what the players endeavour to do.' He continues: 'Players are very cultured people and should be treated with a sense of humanity – essential in a twenty-first century conductor.' Like Nona Liddell he considers it a priority 'to make an orchestra feel at ease. The time when charisma was an essential ingredient of a conductor's persona has gone. Self-governing orchestras will no longer accept Toscanini-like childishness. Electricity comes from a conductor's gestural language, as with Hans Rosbaud.' Joel Sachs offers a similar warning to 'avoid ego trips. You are not there to show how great you are.' There is a clear warning from these comments. In the twenty-first century conductors cannot behave like divas. Orchestras will not tolerate those who do. Sachs extends the point: 'and will probably become demoralised if their management forces it upon them'.

Ross Pople favours a conductor 'who is non-combative – one who encourages an orchestra to give. An approach based on a concept of "the orchestra and me" is unproductive; it should be simply "us". Ego gets in the way of any creative act.' I consider the last remark to have profound resonance in the response of any orchestral musician.

The issue of co-ordination of large forces, especially when a chorus is involved, produces diverse approaches from conductors. Some consider the comparative distance of the chorus from the conductor compared with the orchestra creates a very small time-lag. The solution they propose is for the orchestra to play with a slightly delayed articulation in relation to the visual beat, as with German orchestras in the past, so that the slightly delayed sound of the chorus can be accommodated. There is historic relevance for this form of beating with Furtwängler, whose manner was designed to produce articulation without an 'edge' from the whole orchestra and the singers. In Wagner this was ideal. In rhythmically more complex music after 1950 it is questionable.

Delayed articulation response to the conductor can also be related to excellent chorus trainers and conductors who are professional organists. In large churches and cathedrals the time lag between articulating the organ keys and the production of the sound can be considerable. This manner of performance sometimes pervades the conducting technique of an organist. I have played with such conductors who can produce brilliant results with such an approach in conventional music. As with Furtwängler, it would be unlikely to work in repertoire with complex rhythmic characteristics.

What *is* questionable is the issue of time lag on the concert hall platform. Manner of articulation is another matter, in that a trombone will have a more 'cushioned' attack than a side-drum. David Purser talks of this as a 'drag approach' to producing a sound, especially in a quiet dynamic. The voice also has a less percussive edge to articulation. With the clarity of gesture recommended by the musicians quoted a conductor's main technical issue in achieving precision from a large orchestra with chorus is the constant manner in which the fall of the beat to the base provides a sense of anticipation for the performers. Precision will result.

In a letter to Councillor Von Mosel Beethoven explains that he has 'often thought of giving up these senseless terms, *Allegro, Andante, Adagio, Presto*, and for this Maelzel's Metronome offers the best opportunity'.[3] The fact that Beethoven gave two differing metronome marks for his Symphony no. 7 leaves us with some uncertainty about the actual tempi he had in mind. But there is enough evidence in Beethoven's letters to indicate the spirit intended in spite of the Italian terminology he finally used. Lionel Friend considers that Beethoven believed his tempo markings when he wrote them, while a performance could have changed his mind. In relation to Wagner he explains that the *Flying Dutchman* and *Tannhäuser* had metronome marks but Wagner soon realised that they didn't work in performance. Leon Botstein makes the same observation about Schumann, 'who made a number of changes'. He explains that Celibidache often took a slower tempo than the one marked because 'he wanted to reveal the inner workings of a piece'. His conclusion is that metronome marks only tell you the composer's intentions as useful indicators, not as an absolute requirement. He qualifies this view using Bartók as an example: 'In performances, Bartók rarely conformed to his own metronome marks.' In the twentieth and twenty-first centuries there have been many recordings which illuminate the flexibility which composers sometimes demonstrate in performances of their own works. Botstein's view is that if the conductor's performance is 'persuasive, no matter what tempo, then it is correct'.

Joel Sachs refers to the two differing editions of *Le Marteau sans maître*, suggesting that in rehearsing the work initially the composer experienced the need for some slower tempi. We have to keep in mind that Boulez often chooses rapid tempi in performances of his own works, especially in later ones such as *Sur incises*. This is particularly characteristic of works which abound in grace-note flourishes. In a discussion with Boulez, Lionel Friend asked about the significance of irregular *sforzandi* within the grace-note groups. Boulez explained that they were there to 'break up the rhythm and its regularity'. Friend considers this 'breaking up of regularity' to be the 'destruction of a sense of pulse – something new'. The relationship between these (in effect)

improvisational characteristics is relative to the huge variety of regular
and irregular pulses in various movements which rely very much on
specific metronome marks. The effect of the whole work is dependant
on adherence to the variable and comparative tempi, controlled by the
metronome marks – and the conductor.

We have seen in Elliott Carter's *Symphony of Three Orchestras* that
the structure of such a work is dependent on metric modulation. With
a conception of this kind I firmly believe that the composer means
what he/she says and that the metronome marks should be observed
exactly. Without such discipline, Carter's work, or Stockhausen's *Gruppen*
for three orchestras with three conductors would simply not work. To
perform such works successfully requires that conductors are able to
determine metronome marks without reference to a metronome. Equally
important is the second requirement – that the conductor must also
generate the spirit of the music as if in Bach or Debussy and avoid any
suggestion of mechanical time-beating, which can never be acceptable.

These observations offer a conclusion that in many cases metronome
marks are only a guide to a composer's intentions and not an absolute.
Some composers will ask for an explicit metronome mark in a live
performance only to find that a recording studio will suggest a
modification. It is only a conductor's sensitivity to the character and
spirit of a work which will make a convincing performance. Joel Sachs
cites Hummel's admonition 'that metronomes be used only to find the
composer's tempo; if they are used while practicing, they make the player
unmusical.' He adds that 'some composers change the markings after
publication. So the printed indications may not be the last word. One
must seek the composer's intention but remain flexible.' As composer
and conductor Mahler resisted putting any metronome marks in any of
his scores, wanting to give the conductor the freedom to assert his/her
own artistry on the performance. Lionel Friend sums up the matter by
quoting Mahler, who suggested that if a metronome mark is chosen by a
conductor for one of his works, it might be right for the first bar.

In learning a new score in preparation for a première a well-developed aural perception is the most important ingredient for a conductor. In the author's experience, both as instrumentalist and composer there are more inadequate performances of premières than of any other category of composition, usually because the conductor's aural perception is so limited that the actual sounds of the score have not been digested, resulting in his/her simply beating time. It took Rachmaninov ten years to discover that his Symphony no. 1 was not a failure, but the victim of a badly performed première. The conductor's ear has an even more demanding task in non-tonal music. For those who are lucky enough to have perfect pitch it is less of an issue. But the process of learning a score is the same as for those who do not have it. The carpet between my desk and my piano is well worn for conducting reasons as well as those of composition. However one chooses to absorb the substance of a new score a highly developed aural perception is the route to a responsible and effective première, not simply a clear conducting technique.

Leon Botstein believes that 'visual score preparation is important'. By that he means that sustaining a visual memory of a page is the foundation for memorising the sounds indicated. He considers that 'most people hear and see the score at the same time. Even people who have photographic memory are still turning pages'. He recommends that 'organising the score in musical sections is valuable'.

Awareness of a conductor's visual needs in the setting of a score is not always understood by some composers. Before computer-set scores became commonplace a conductor would usually have to read from a manuscript copy, even if the work was published. In most cases these scores were prepared with immaculate graphic clarity (works of art in themselves) by composers who sustained a sense of responsibility towards the conductor. At other times the conductor has to do a good deal of rewriting. We have to keep in mind that before composers did their own settings by computer, most premières were performed before the publication of a printed setting. In my own experience computer-set scores by composers who are not entirely expert create more problems than manuscript scores, no matter how good the compositions might be. In a large orchestral score a composer might choose to put all instruments on individual staves, rather than coupling the woodwind and horn parts where possible. When divided strings are added, the result can be a score that is too small to read properly. My solution to this has sometimes been to make an enlarged photocopy and use a cardboard extension for the music stand to accommodate the overlarge score. The composer's and/or publisher's permission to do this is required; but it is unlikely that publishers would provide such a score. If a composer chooses to put time-signatures on each stave rather than enlarged ones at section subdivisions, quite an operation is needed if there are multiple time changes. Pencilling them in is quite a task. Whether manuscript or computer set, marking cues and rewriting metric marks, if too small, can be part of the score learning process. Using abbreviations or even single letters to identify instrumental cues might be underlined with a diagonal line – a distinctive angle which belongs to no musical symbol. Joel Sachs goes even further by 'marking scores with coloured pens' if he owns the scores. He marks all metric changes and highlights dynamics. His view that 'dramaturgy is the most important part of learning a score' illustrates the importance he attaches to perceiving the character of a new work at the outset and the colours help him to see the dramaturgy clearly. Leon Botstein recommends that a new score should be marked up in the same way as a conventional one, especially if a conductor does not have photographic memory. He considers that even in the chance scores of Morton Feldman he 'finds ways of organising events in sequences of boxes'. On the question of managing transformation and repetition in the minimalist scores of Steve Reich or John Adams he sees the conductor's role as 'finding a structural analysis of such music'. Anthony Payne is less positive about minimalist music. He recognises that the reactionary attitude by many composers to the complexity established by the Darmstadt composers had merit. Minimalism was an example of this 'easing up, if rather childish'. He continues: 'It was a commercial road in substance resulting in dull material lacking in mature emotion.' There might be some conductors who share this view, but it is still their responsibility to perform it if required. If so, developing a temporary enthusiasm for it is to be applied.

Following any graphic additions if required in a score, Joel Sachs suggests that 'working at the gestures forms part of the process of learning it while reserving the need to make changes in rehearsal, if the need arises.' There are many composers who readily admit that conducting is not what they do and therefore, have no pretensions on the matter. There are, of course, many works in which the composer does not wish to have rhythmic consistency from one performance to another. The distinctive graphics for this concept, as in Lutosławski, are discussed in Part One. Lionel Friend uses Peter Maxwell Davies as an example of a composer 'who will write a triplet within a triplet'. He finds this 'difficult to rationalise in performance. With Carter you have to do the arithmetic because the notation is rational, if complex. Exact displacement of notes is essential for him.' The difference between two such composers 'is a matter of style' is Friend's conclusion.

When improvisational characteristics form the substance of a composition, as was discussed in Maderna's *Giardino religioso* (p. 60), Friend has a warning to composers if they simply 'tell players to do what they like'. While Maderna does not do that in so many words, an improvisational element can be interpreted with sarcasm by a performer who might be unconvinced by the music. Bigotry is an attitude conductors have to deal with. Friend had to confront it when rehearsing Maderna's work. 'The horn player interpreted an improvisational instruction by playing the horn solo from *Till Eulenspiegel*!' Friend thinks that 'such instructions are successful when a whole work is conceived improvisationally, with elaborate explanations on how it should be played, as in Cage'. Joel Sachs maintains that 'a composer is innocent until proven guilty. We have to start by trusting the composer.' Friend supports such a view, even when a composer oversteps the boundaries of reasonable interpretation. 'If the music is good, you have to try to realise the composer's intentions, even if there are sometimes extreme demands.'

I hold the view that in all generations of composers the number of less worthy compositions far outstrips the number of masterpieces. An ensemble specialising in performing contemporary music will encounter works in the same proportion. With this in mind it can sometimes be disconcerting for players in performing such a mix. Therefore it is

necessary for the conductor to empathise with the mind-set of a good
instrumentalist or singer who experiences doubts with a confession that
he/she does not understand a work. Such doubts are exposed in a journal
article of 1980 by a young clarinettist, Antony Pay.[4] He is an extremely
intelligent musician who worked with the London Sinfonietta at the time.
There is great integrity in what he says: 'As performers we are often in
the worst position to have a clear idea of what is going on in a piece. This
isn't confined to the music of our time, of course; but it has to be said
that such music is often complex, which adds to the problem. And when
one takes into account that we are tied up with the difficulty of what we
have to play, and that *few conductors put over any developed sense of the style
of a new work, it's not surprising that we often feel at a loss* [my italics].'

I consider Lionel Friend to be one of the 'few conductors' who do
convey the substance and style of a new work in rehearsal. He recognises
that players respond to words of enthusiasm from a conductor, especially
if they are revealing about the structure and substance of a work. He
holds the view that even a display of excitement will be reflected by the
performers' responses if the conductor demonstrates an authoritative
understanding of a work. He stresses the importance of 'trying to look at
every piece from the composer's point of view'. There are so many issues
in a good work which go beyond the written page. A composer cannot
put everything in the score. It is up to the conductor to sustain a constant
search for yet more detail.

Nona Liddell considers it to be 'absolutely necessary to have sectional
rehearsals in this repertoire, even with a small ensemble'. As a leader she
finds that details of bowing and phrasing can be settled more quickly, so
that full rehearsal will not involve time-wasting discussion, while leaving
enough scope if changes become necessary. She also adds that parts
must be sent to all players in advance of the rehearsal schedule. These
collaborative arrangements contribute to the success of a première, she
concludes.

When a conductor has prepared a new score in detail before a first
full rehearsal, David Hockings has experienced those conductors 'who
are unwilling to respond to requests from players, especially when
involving the multi-tasks of the percussion section'. This could be for
changing the order of irregular beats, a request for a subdivision of

beats or to leave more temporal space for a rush of grace notes to be manageable. He considers this to be a matter of courtesy, making it possible for the players to respond to the complex issues of so much new music. To show this kind of respect for the players will achieve respect for the conductor and create a feeling of mutual confidence. Hockings continues: 'In allowing players, especially percussionists, to work with their own initiative always wins the best performances.' He thinks that 'By responding to requests positively, a good working collaboration can be established quickly.' It is his firm belief that this is a good tenet for all conductors. Hockings is also critical of conductors who stop too often in rehearsal, giving the players no chance to get to know their parts or to become familiar with the substance of a new work. I consider this to be an essential principle in rehearsing any kind of music. The conductor should collate rehearsal issues in his/her mind while playing through a work and deal with these several issues directly and succinctly when a section is completed.

Lionel Friend sustains an interesting affection for 'composers who don't care too much about the excessive practical demands they make on performers'. Beethoven is an obvious example of this in the persistently high register in the chorus parts of the Ninth Symphony. Friend thinks that, like other composers who are sometimes excessive in their challenges, 'he simply wrote what he wanted to hear. Michael Tippett wrote quite impossible things sometimes, but the conductor has to find a solution – he/she has to try.' This is a generous defence by Friend of the questing composer, which exemplifies the positive determination a conductor should demonstrate in rehearsing a work that contains eccentric characteristics which might well finish up seeming inspired, once learned by an orchestra. This admirable integrity was totally inappropriate in one work in which Friend was painstakingly seeking perfection in a rehearsal of an early work by Penderecki. The composer complained that he didn't want it to sound the same in every performance. 'It's meant to sound like chaos!' Penderecki shouted. Friend's admiration for composers who have experimented in this way reflects the philosophy which many composers adopted in Penderecki's early years. 'An idea could be expressed which did not require an interpretation' is how Friend puts it. Irregular pulse had spread to irregularity of note displacements in these works.

'Interpretation' is a word which Stravinsky questioned in his 1935 *Autobiography*. This raises the semantic issue of how to interpret 'interpretation' in the context of Stravinsky's statement. Even Schoenberg's distaste for vibrato did not invalidate the importance of a performer's subjective artistry as an essential ingredient in the performance of any music. Stravinsky's admiration for Ernest Ansermet's artistry indicates that such subjectivity is acceptable for him if it does not involve the indulgence of ego. A debate on this would involve wide ramifications. Sufficient to say that there is irony in the fact that in Stravinsky's memorial service Bernstein conducted the 'Glorification de l'élue' and 'Danse sacrale' in an edited version with *regular* pulse notation. David Purser was the bass-trumpet soloist in this performance and found it difficult to play because he knew the authentic version so well. What he found interesting was that Bernstein began the rehearsal with the 'Danse sacrale' and spent quite some time talking about the music and its intricacy. Regularly employed as the bass-trumpeter in the work, Purser was particularly impressed by the rehearsal process of Boulez. Intonation and detail were addressed to all sections of the orchestra and the chords at the beginning of Part 2 were 'stripped down' and analysed, so that all the players knew how their own parts were reflected in the whole. Purser reflects on the distinctive interpretations he experienced with three different conductors performing Birtwistle's *Secret Theatre*. He recalls that each of them created differing results – but all good. To reiterate Boulez: 'To imitate the gestures of other conductors is completely useless …'

The vocal soloist in this repertoire has the most forbidding task of all musicians. With no tonic to relate to and rhythmic complexity to secure, there is little to hold on to except the conductor's direction. Jane Manning's vast repertoire, with hundreds of premières in her catalogue of performances, makes her a supreme authority on the subject. While she is complimentary about certain conductors she is also critical of those who show no understanding of the specific concerns of a vocal soloist. She stresses that 'The most important issue is breathing. If a conductor has not absorbed the substance and *pacing* of a new work there is a danger that the tempo can slacken to the point where a singer will run out of breath.' She has experienced this even with notable conductors who do not seem to be able to empathise with vocal performance requirements. This is by no means an issue related only to contemporary music. Wagner warned that conductors 'cannot find the true tempo because they are ignorant of singing. ... These people look upon music as a singularly abstract sort of thing, an amalgam of grammar, arithmetic and digital gymnastics'.[5] Manning uses less abrasive words to make the same observation about conductors who do not possess enough flexibility in their technique of directing to accommodate breathing. 'A conductor should *not* interfere with a soloist's pacing and style. He/she should allow the singer to lead like a good piano accompanist, who will simply *be with* the soloist.' While Manning thinks that a conductor 'must *feel* all of this' the beating manner which conveys anticipation is the key to 'making a singer feel comfortable'. Without such an approach the conductor can 'make easy passages feel difficult' adding to the difficulties which a score might possess for a singer.

These observations take issue with conductors who are unaware of the practicalities which inhibit an effective performance from singers. Manning is also critical of singers who do not prepare their parts sufficiently. As an artist who is widely known to be note-perfect at every rehearsal she has little patience with singers who fail in this regard because conductors often spend a disproportionate amount of rehearsal time dealing with their problems rather than the musical results. A conductor should avoid such a situation because it limits the time available for singers who *do* prepare their performances adequately. Manning's recommendation is that conductors should make provision for 'prior rehearsal time for singers who require coaching'. This underlines the special difficulties which relate to singers in non-tonal music. She quotes a conductor who ignored one of the solo singers in a rehearsal who was not properly prepared. When she asked him why he had done this he replied: 'I don't want to waste time on people who can't do it.' This implied that his priority was to get the best performance from those who *could* do it' and could benefit from rehearsal time well spent. Good advice!

As a singer who performed in Stockhausen's *Donnerstag* from the *Licht* cycle of operas, Julian Pike does not favour any methodology for singers in performing music which travels outside diatonic language. He recognises that composers have been wary of choosing rhythmic complexity in addition to non-tonal substance as an element in their operas for this reason. Benjamin Britten, Hans Werner Henze, György Ligeti, George Benjamin and many others seem to recognise the multi-tasking requirements of the opera singer and usually sustain regular units in the vocal substance of their operatic works. Pike believes in singers 'simply getting used to it' when difficulties arise. For the conductor he points to the issues of concern for the opera singer. The singers can sustain confidence in such works if the conductor 'manifests awareness of all the things which a singer has to think about on stage, especially the correlation of acting with the singing role. Eye-contact is not always possible between conductor and singer – an aspect which must be understood. So the conductor has to be sensitive to a singer's movements.' My recommendations about the manner of lifting the beat slower than the fall, is one way of assuring this sensitised cohesion. Pike takes the point further 'Once production arrangements are in place a good conductor, like a good accompanist, will allow opera singers to do as they wish with the music. If this creates a problem initially in matters of style, a process of persuasion works best, not demand. In coaching sessions it is good to keep in mind that conductors don't sing, so they should not interfere with a singer's technique.' Jane Manning underlines this by stating that 'interfering with a vocal manner results in making matters worse. Creating confidence is of vital importance in coaching singers either in opera or in concert performance. If *rubato* is an element of a work, especially in interpreting complex music in the concert repertoire, a manner of flexibility must be established by the conductor to allow a solo singer to dictate the expressive use of such freedom'. An illustration of this point is discussed in Part Three, relating to movement 3 of Boulez's *Le Marteau sans maître* (p. 160), which is performed in entirety on the accompanying DVD track 5.

Choral groups serve several different kinds of composition, from large oratorios with orchestra to four-part *a cappella* works. The line between amateur and professional singers involved is very thin, except for the wholly professional ensembles, such as the BBC Singers. David Wordsworth (a pianist who conducts an *a cappella* choir) insists that a conductor should 'never treat amateurs as amateurs'. This good advice informs all that we now discuss. Wordsworth considers choral conducting and orchestral conducting to be two distinctive disciplines, even to the point of using a baton when an orchestra is involved, but never for an *a cappella* performance. He maintains that 'It is possible for an orchestra to manage without cues or eye-contact, whereas a choir is totally dependent on both aspects.' This feature was illustrated in the performance of a twentieth-century work involving the BBC Chorus 'who expressed devastation that they were given no cues and the conductor didn't look at them once'. Wordsworth explains that a conductor 'has to be with a chorus *all* the time'. Timothy Salter (a composer and conductor of an *a cappella* choir) extends this important issue by pointing out that 'an instrumentalist reads from a single part for the instrument, whereas choirs have to use scores. While the latter provides printed cues they must also be signalled from the conductor if uncertainty is to be avoided.' He has a different point of view from Wordsworth in believing that the technique of conducting is the same for a chorus as an orchestra, in that the same issues arise for chorus and orchestra in this kind of repertoire. My conclusion is that either approach will work if the technique adopted projects the authority and control required.

Salter's experience is that he finds it easier for a choir to sustain secure pitch in non-tonal music than in diatonic works, because in the latter intonation tends to drift more easily. This can be a problem for singers who have perfect pitch.

Training a choir is obviously the responsibility of a chorus master, whether he/she conducts the performance or someone else, which is often the case when a professional orchestra is involved. Salter points out that a chorus master responsible for the training 'can be in conflict with the performance conductor. The mannerisms of the "guest" conductor can be difficult for a choir to adapt to.' Salter specifies that 'too small a window of activity in the geometry of the beat, or a fluttering hand, can be confusing'. Wordsworth stresses a basic issue often overlooked by the concert conductor: 'Getting attention at the beginning is important. Choirs can bury their heads in the score so must be encouraged to sing at least the first three bars from memory. In the training process learning a piece from memory can contribute enormously to the quality of a performance.' One work he uses for this purpose is Mozart's *Ave verum corpus*. This 'gets the singers into the habit of watching the conductor as much as possible'. Salter underlines this with a recommendation to the guest conductor always to be clear in cueing an entry so that a breath can be taken at the right moment. 'Breathing with an upbeat can be inappropriate in a fast passage. The preparation for a cue must allow in a measured way for the choir to take a breath.' He continues: 'If the entry is on a high note the conductor's gesture must be relaxed, so that the singers will not be tense in production.' This is, of course, equally true for the orchestra in avoiding an accentuated response. 'Singers can be encouraged to think of the bow on the string to avoid an explosive articulation.'

Wordsworth confronts the issue of sustaining pitch in a work which diverges from notated pitches to non-pitched sounds. This occurs in Sven-David Sandström's *Hear my Prayer, O Lord*, based on a verse anthem by Purcell. 'The first response of the singers is that it looks difficult. Once they have found pitch reference points they should get away from the piano as soon as possible.' Wordsworth stresses the importance of this 'psychological reaction' to a challenging work like the Sandström or Berio's *Passaggio*, stressing that 'Singers are intelligent, cultured people who respond well to intelligent training – not bullying!' He adds that 'Your confidence will give them confidence.' 'The enthusiasm of amateurs should be fed' is how Julian Pike stresses the need for a conductor to have a psychological awareness of the mind-set of people who love to sing in a choir.

In sharing these views of the training process Salter extends the points in relation to the need for the performance conductor being involved at some stage. He goes as far as to say that in a work like Stockhausen's *Carré*, which involves four large ensembles and choruses, 'All four conductors should participate in the early rehearsals, because voices are part of the ensemble – not separate.' In relation to the characterisation of a work he recommends that 'works which involve layered textures which create 'cloud' of chords such as Jonathan Harvey's *Come Holy Ghost*, vibrato should be avoided. 'The dissonances involved need clarity of intonation to be effective.' At the same time, 'Vitality of the sound must always be present.' Wordsworth offers good advice on rehearsal procedure: 'Finish on a high! Rehearse the most difficult sections in the middle of the rehearsal, but don't concentrate too long on them. Providing food for thought can be a useful complement to hard work and will avoid creating tension.'

In the opera house Jane Manning and Julian Pike have concerns about some conductors who seem to have an inflated sense of their own importance. While recognising the need for authority to be shown, they insist that the conductor should constantly remind him/herself that the music comes from the singers and the players. Their expertise should be acknowledged. In issues of interpretation, pacing or *rubato* they say that a conductor can learn from singers and should not assume that they don't know about the contextualisation of their own roles in the complete work. Such knowledge should be 'treated with respect'. Both singers have wide experience of performing and recording the progressive music of their own time and their views on conductors *and* composers are well founded. Manning considers Boulez's vocal writing to be sensitively conceived for voice in practical as well as in applying an aesthetic realisation of the poetry used. She considers the clarity of balancing the vocal parts with an ensemble or orchestra are beautifully realised in his scoring. Recognising that Stockhausen was quite a contentious composer in his own lifetime and suffered quite a lot of abuse from some critics, Pike considers him to have been 'a genius'. He says that 'his sound-world was unique

and sustained with great integrity against so much adverse criticism'.
Conductors who respect such views will achieve the best performances.

☐ ☐ ☐ ☐

When Giuseppe di Giugno's pioneering work in electronics opened the pathway to interactive techniques, he was sympathetic to the limitations of many conductors who had no training in electronics. 'Synthesizers should be made for musicians, not [for] the people that make them' was one of his goals – and good news for conductors who can take advantage of his innovations. But this does not reduce the number of issues which he/she must deal with in rehearsal and performance. While conductors do not need to be involved in the technology related to works deploying live instruments and computers, their awareness of the often complex tasks of those controlling the electronic element is vital, especially in rehearsals. Lamberto Coccioli was an assistant to Luciano Berio for several years and presided over the electronics in many performances of the composer's works. He offers a number of recommendations for conductors who have no training in electro-acoustic music. The information in Part One (p. 81) relating to several works is a useful introduction to his comments.

Coccioli considers that balance is the most difficult issue for a conductor to deal with because he/she is not in the right position to listen to the combined effect of the electro-acoustic element through the speakers around the auditorium and the live instruments which might also be amplified. His solution to this is that a second conductor should be available in rehearsals so that the main conductor can listen to the effect in the auditorium. This would be a useful experience for a student. The more complex a synthesizer the more difficult it is to adapt their use to analogue works. This is also affected by their rather speedy obsolescence and the fact that they cannot be replaced once new models have entered the market.

The title describing the person who controls the electronic element in a performance was originally 'sound engineer'. Coccioli prefers 'electronics performer' as a more appropriate description. With 'real time' works of this kind Coccioli thinks it wise for a pre-rehearsal to be devoted to those involved with the electronics. It is important for the electronics performer to have a major input relating to the format for rehearsals. The issue of balance will then be mutually understood, saving time when the instrumentalists arrive. He recommends the use of a monitor speaker near the conductor in some works where it can help to give him/her a clearer idea of the total sound.

For a conductor performing such works for the first time Coccioli makes some recommendations. Some scores use symbols for treatments such as band-filtering. It is important to know what basic diagrams mean. Live electronic interactions design is more complex, but should be studied. Some composers include a great deal of information about the electronic element in their scores. They must be studied and digested so that discussions with the electronics performer can be fruitful. In analogue days there were several assistants required for a performance. The software that has been developed replaces them and cannot be designed without some complexity involved. Therefore, it is important for the conductor to allow the electronics performer to 'call the shots' initially. There are so many things to check before all the elements can be brought together.

Many works with live electronics use a list of cues that correspond to discrete electronic events. Cues are triggered by the electronics performer. In rehearsal any cue can be chosen by the conductor if the number is clearly given to the electronics performer operating them. As stated in Part One, in performance the cue must be anticipated with a raised left arm a few seconds before conveying the signal on the appropriate beat. For reasons already stated, the conductor must always have in mind that the electronics performer has a fairly complicated task, not only in setting up, but in performing the required operations in rehearsal and performance. Technical faults can occur. When this happens a conductor must not complain – and might use the time either rehearsing the orchestra or explaining what the music is about if it is a première. The more the players know about a work the more they can apply their artistry to the performance.

Coccioli offers some final words of advice. When organising rehearsals make sure that lots of time is provided for the electronics performer to set up. Nothing can be rushed. Cables and leads from instrument microphones will pass through the orchestral seating. This might be a new consideration for some players. So they should be warned to take care to avoid standing on them or, even worse, placing a cello spike on one! At every opportunity explain what the music is about. It is not always understood by instrumentalists that the electronic element is an integrated part of the score and not a separate element. Encourage the players to think of the electronics as a musical instrument . After all, in electronically prerecorded tapes, the sound sources are often treated live instruments. Coccioli encourages conductors to accept that after what can be an exhausting process of rehearsal in which the electronics performer has to be involved in many of the decisions, it is the conductor who must take the final responsibility. Such collaboration is the mainstay of this exciting and evolving medium.

While readers will be fully aware of the practical issues related to a conductor's responsibilities there are some matters in the percussion arena which require special attention. The variety and number of instruments deployed in various scores is a constant challenge to the players, who often have to go well beyond the call of duty to fulfil their role. David Hockings explains these issues. He recounts an experience in which the conductor had no concern for the special needs of the section. The work was Boulez's *Rituel,* but the conductor was not the composer. After spending a great deal of time waiting for the hired instruments to arrive for the first rehearsal, the conductor did not rehearse the piece. The dress rehearsal was the only occasion when there was a complete play-through – for 15 minutes! Added to this, the conductor gave no consideration for the setting-up time needed. With such a lack of concern and an absence of understanding of these practicalities the result was 'chaos in the performance'. Hockings concluded that the conductor had no interest in the music and did not know how to deal with the score, choosing *not* to deal with its requirements. Such an experience also demonstrated the conductor's failure to understand that such a work is not known to any of the players as much as a work of, say, Ravel. The players require much more rehearsal time than they do in a well-known work. Percussion players have so many more practical issues to deal with than any other section of the orchestra in this kind of repertoire.

Hockings has also experienced conductors who show little concern for the varying combination of instruments in each of several works in one programme. Each station might require a different combination of instruments from one work to another. Whenever the pieces are adjacent in a programme, this requires time to reorganise, *which must be specified by the players.* Rather than having a break of 10–15 minutes between each piece the conductor and concert organisers would be well advised to confer with the percussion section regarding what order of programme would work best to avoid such breaks between performances in the concert. If an alternative cannot be found, Hockings recommends providing a discussion for the audience about the works to be performed.

Whatever is decided it must be understood that setting up cannot be hurried.

Another consideration for the conductor in such a programme concerns the number of players and their numbered order in the score. The conductor might prepare a new score with five percussionists involved, thinking that the stations will be ordered 1–5 from left to right on the platform. Arranging a vast number of sometimes heavy instruments in the most convenient manner players might have to change the numerical order from left to right from one piece to another, so that player no. 1 in the score might have to be placed in the middle of the section. The conductor should make note of this in consultation with the players. Sometimes percussionists have to share instruments in a single station, so that they will not always be in the same place on the platform. Halls will also vary in dictating how the stations must be set up. A conductor must always adapt to the decisions of the players and not insist on a convenient arrangement for him/herself. Without their input on logistics required, the players will experience unnecessary problems which will adversely affect the performance. All of these recommendations are provided by David Hockings.

A responsible conductor will have decided on the beating directions of a complex work before the first rehearsal and marked up the score. However, some flexibility in rehearsal is needed for players who request an alternative beating pattern in, for instance, irregular pulses. If the request is reasonable and does not adversely affect other players, it should be accepted. It might be said that some players can be obstructive in addressing such decisions. Good-natured persuasion is the only response worth pursuing.

▢ ▢ ▢ ▢

Techniques for training and conducting a youth or college orchestra are covered in Christopher Adey's excellent book *Orchestral Performance*.[6] Some of the interviewees already quoted in Part Two of this book contribute further considerations.

Colleges and conservatoires occasionally invite a distinguished professional conductor to rehearse and conduct a concert with the students. Some achieve excellent performances, providing a valuable and memorable experience for the young performers. Others fail to engage with an orchestra, resulting in a tense and inadequate performance. From observations, my own conclusion is that a lack of teaching experience usually accounts for this failure, no matter how accomplished the conductor might be. Expectations from a professional orchestra are based on the expertise and experience of the orchestral musicians, plus the assumption that they can tackle anything put in front of them. If a conductor carries this assumption in rehearsing with the comparatively inexperienced musicians in a college, frustration will be mutual for the students and the conductor. Rehearsals with students of any standard should be based on teaching them, whether on technical issues or artistic perception. In conducting complex contemporary orchestral works with students I have always found them receptive to instruction and guidance if patience, determination and a little humour are the supportive ingredients. No matter how unsatisfactory the efforts of individual students might be, they must never be humiliated in the presence of the orchestra. This can be psychologically damaging as well as unfair and unproductive.

While these comments might seem unnecessary observations which can be taken for granted, it is surprising how often the fallibility of human nature makes us overlook such issues. I consider them to be strict rules in a conductor s responsibilities. Leon Botstein brings the student conductor into these issues with observations relating to college and university courses. In judging a student performance he feels that 'too much emphasis can be placed on what a conductor looks like and not enough on what the result sounds like.' While this is a generalisation, he has witnessed this as an adjudicator in conducting competitions where

'The criteria are based on appearance and manner rather than artistry.' In relation to the aural training of a conducting student, the perception required for non-tonal music is much wider than that for diatonic works. Botstein thinks that 'students listening to recordings is no substitute for the empirical process of conceiving the sound of a score from the page'. David Purser believes that 'Weak aural perception is partly due to the excessive reliance on a computer rather than working out sound combinations at the keyboard and practising the results.' He continues: 'This point aside, music courses provide a good balance between practical and academic study.' How far this should be taken brings us back to Boulez's belief that 'teachers of composition and conducting ought to be in the same boat.'[7] Joel Sachs maintains that 'the theoretical knowledge gained by studying composition is absolutely necessary for a conductor'. Botstein has the same opinion: 'A conductor has to think like a composer. The ability to present constructive analysis is vital.' From the composer's point of view Anthony Payne agrees that 'The conductors who perform contemporary music with real understanding are usually those who can compose as well.' Erich Leinsdorf goes even further when he insists that 'All those who wish to study with me should have a comprehensive knowledge of composition.'[8]

Nona Liddell presents a violinist's opinion: 'Regardless of whether or not conductors can compose, if the rehearsal of a complex work includes comments on analysis and background to provide enlightened observations about the music and its expression, players approve.'

▢ ▢ ▢ ▢

In creating a programme which features new music, initially we have the issue of diversity in style to consider. As in other eras there is also the wide range of quality from disastrous music to masterpieces to put into the equation. On both points we have the subjective element of personal preferences involved. Nonetheless, there are enough objective criteria to assert in the matter of judging what constitutes an accomplished work of art. When sitting on adjudication panels I am always interested to identify jury members who have a reasoned approach to judgement in balancing the subjective with the objective and those who veer towards wholly subjective. In assessing the qualities of a composition this balance is of vital importance in choosing the works which can result in an interesting concert. What will attract a wide range of concert-goers must go into the choices as well. A further question involves the aspirations of individual composers. What kind of audience do they compose *for*? A composer of integrity will reply that he/she has respect for the individuality of each member of an audience, not classes of taste. Therefore, it is not possible to compose *for* an audience. The composer can only express in the music what he/she feels to be a valid statement of artistic endeavour and hope that it will find resonance in some members of an audience. With these questions in mind as a starting point, a compelling programme will be dependent simply on a good idea.

There is common agreement that 'ghettoising' new music simply isolates it from potential audiences. Leon Botstein believes that programmes devoted entirely to new music 'can create a fear and uneasiness in an audience'. He urges strongly that 'young conductors especially must not fall prey to it'. He suggests that a 'transparent logic' should be asserted in creating a programme. 'A formal structure which contains comparable musical attributes is a good starting point', is how he puts it. In an orchestral concert the following choices might be made: a work by a composer who studied with Elliott Carter, a work by Carter himself, and one by Edgard Varèse. The 'logic' behind such a programme would be Carter's French association with his teacher Nadia Boulanger and the French/American connection with Varèse. If the work by Carter's pupil, Tod Machover, was *Sparkler* for orchestra and interactive computer electronics, this would cement the relationship in the programme because Machover worked extensively at IRCAM in Paris and studied with Carter in the USA. Botstein's 'comparable musical attributes' would be applied even more intensively if Carter was represented by his Oboe Concerto, which was composed for Heinz Holliger, a composition pupil of Boulez. With Varèse's *Arcana* the resulting programme would be a mosaic of contrasts emanating from a common source – but with immense variety. The mixture of three generations of composers also avoids an exclusively contemporary programme.

Joel Sachs feels that the problem of audience response is most acute at new music concerts. 'At such a programme, if each audience member comes away having responded very strongly (positively) to at least one piece, that is good. With sufficient variety of styles a programme of unfamiliar music is likely to be much more persuasive.' Like Botstein, he believes in constantly looking for new composers to set against more familiar works. 'Ensembles can be taken over by their seriousness' is a comment from him which is a good caveat for any ensemble that specialises in performing contemporary music.

Botstein thinks that an audience can be drawn by 'mixing the cultures'. Painting and music in the 1950s in USA is one of his suggestions. In planning a concert of UK music he avoids the obvious choices of Britten and Tippett in preference for Frank Bridge set against later composers. David Purser addresses the subject of attracting a wide audience with the issue of 'charismatic conductors' admired by a wide public, who are bold enough to mix their programmes with complex contemporary music with standard classics. Daniel Barenboim took a huge step in this direction by featuring Boulez and Beethoven in six consecutive concerts at BBC Promenade Concerts in 2012. The vast audience, many of whom would have been there for Beethoven, might have heard Boulez for the first time as a revelatory experience.

In the eighteenth and nineteenth centuries audiences were accustomed to expect new works and music of their own time in any concert. The question arises: why should Boulez and Beethoven in the same programme be such an exceptional event? The ability for a conductor to develop a capacity to conduct music of all periods underlies the technical and artistic recommendations made throughout this book. The study of Italian and French ornamentation in the baroque era is not a specialist preoccupation. It is part of the framework in the stylistic evolution of musical language, in the same way that studying the composition techniques of Wagner or Messiaen is essential to the interpretation of their music. A programme which spans these epochs will find an enquiring audience. David Wordsworth provides a remark which signifies this holistic concept of programming: 'Don't do Tallis if you can't do modern. One can be as difficult as the other', a leavening comment which the author fully endorses.

Collating the comments of a variety of musicians has produced significant agreement on the main issues a conductor has to confront in relation to his/her responsibilities to new and contemporary music. It is a pivotal role which he/she plays in interpreting to the orchestra or ensemble the language of each composer after 1950, then bringing the works to life for an audience. Each stage requires an intellectual and artistic commitment which is best driven by passion.

□ □ □ □

PART THREE
Case studies

In order to get the most from Part Three the reader will need to have the scores to hand and refer to them constantly.

Pierre Boulez, *Le Marteau sans maître*

Score: Universal Edition, 1957

The amount of authoritative literature available on this work, including Boulez's own writings, makes it unnecessary to enter into further detailed discussion about its historical significance and structural organisation. But where appropriate to issues of conducting, such matters will be referred to. Score references relate to the 1957 Universal Edition.

In the journey which he made from the strict serialism and the 'automatism'[1] of *Structure I* (1951) to *Le Marteau sans maître* (1954), Boulez made a giant leap of inventive perception. The composer himself describes the earlier work as a purely technical exploration of musical language 'to bring everything into question again, make a clean sweep of one's heritage and start all over again from scratch, to see how it might be possible to reconstruct a way of writing that begins with something which eliminates personal invention'.[2] He is not out of step with many and diverse composers who see the material of a piece sometimes dictating its own direction. Finding a balance between subjective input and the independent life of a musical construct is common ground for many composers. What Boulez was seeking in *Le Marteau* was an aesthetic determinant produced by the *flexible* function of composition technique, 'local indiscipline'[3] as he describes it. Serialism, as conceived in the Darmstadt years, became for him a 'fetishism of numbers' which he describes as 'banal'.[4] This is an extremely important observation for any conductor who is learning and preparing the work for performance. In an interview with Boulez during his seventy-fifth birthday celebrations, I asked him what had determined his path from the strict application of serialism in *Structure I* to the exotic world of *Le Marteau*. I quote his reply: 'When I was a student I wrote canons and fugues. Now I am not a student I do not write canons and fugues!'

This explanation underlines a misconception in many history books, concerning the significance of serial techniques in the evolution of musical language in the twentieth century. It was a very brief investigation by young composers in a post-war period of renewal. An illustration of this can be seen in successive works of Stockhausen, in which a new concept is asserted in each piece. The same can be said of

Berio, Nono and others. And so it was with Boulez. The sound world of *Le Marteau* must be conceived by a conductor with the *textural* result of such musical organisation, not least in relation to the fact that apart from the two movements which deploy all of the ensemble, each of the other movements contains differing combinations of the six instruments and voice. This is related to the structural concept in which three of Char's poems are integrated into three cycles: 'L'Artisanat furieux' is a three-movement cycle; 'Bourreaux de solitude' has four movements; 'Bel édifice et les pressentiments' has two. The movements of each cycle interlock and interpenetrate each other so that there is a sense of interruption in each cycle until the final movement which, in Boulez's own words 'is a microcosm of the entire work'.[5]

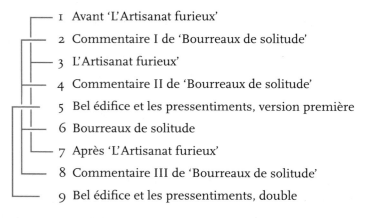

1 Avant 'L'Artisanat furieux'

2 Commentaire I de 'Bourreaux de solitude'

3 L'Artisanat furieux'

4 Commentaire II de 'Bourreaux de solitude'

5 Bel édifice et les pressentiments, version première

6 Bourreaux de solitude

7 Après 'L'Artisanat furieux'

8 Commentaire III de 'Bourreaux de solitude'

9 Bel édifice et les pressentiments, double

I refer readers to the composer's own discussion of the work in Boulez's essay 'Speaking, Playing, Singing',[6] where he describes the vocal part as a compliment to the flute, where roles reverse in no. 9 when the vocal line becomes wordless and the flute takes over the role. The final section of this movement is taken over by percussion and flute in one of the most moving and expressive codas in the repertoire. Boulez describes the poem as 'being at the *centre* of the music though it is in fact *absent* from the music'.[7] With such a perspective the practical preparation can begin.

Seating plan

Seating the performers in an effective formation is important. Boulez recommends the following:[8]

Percussion

Xylophone   Vibraphone

Guitar   Singer

Viola   Flute

This formation is based on perceptions of balance and keeping the vocal line integrated with the ensemble, so that the reversal of the flute and singer roles in no. 9 can be successful. My own experience in conducting the work presents an alternative. Having experimented with the Boulez formation the singer in the ensemble (Alison Wells, with whom I have performed the work several times) found it unacceptable to have the flute directed towards her throughout the work. Another consideration is that the flute is directing the sound away from the audience. My own solution is as follows:

Percussion   Xylophone   Vibraphone

Singer   Viola

Flute   Guitar

With this arrangement the flute becomes a soloist in no. 9, while the singer is still integrated into the formation. The composer's requirement is still fulfilled in that the singer is 'able either to stand out as soloist or to retire into anonymity when replaced by the flute'.[9] With the guitar closer to the audience and the viola facing the audience, both positions are beneficial acoustically. The percussion being slightly at the side provides closer contact with the flute in their coda duo.

The first issue to consider in the music is metronome marks. There is a wide discrepancy between the very fast tempi instructions of the first edition (1954) and the second (1957). At the opening of the first movement the editions read respectively ♩ = 208 and ♩ = 168. Up to this time no conductor had been required to conduct a unit over 170. Part Three, section 3 explains how even a tempo of up to 252 can be conducted in music which requires exactly that speed of direction (DVD track 2). So Boulez is by no means asking too much of a conductor to direct at ♩ = 208. In the second movement the respective speeds are ♩ = 76 and ♩ = 60. For the instrumentalist the faster tempi are not excessive in relation to the technical facility required, a fact that is illustrated in Boulez's own recordings of the work. It has to be borne in mind that in relation to the xylophone and vibraphone the use of four rather than two mallets is common today. This was not the case when the piece was composed. Disregarding this factor, a careful examination of the motivic structure of the score will expose the fact that speed of articulation is rare in any of the nine movements. The challenges arise in the independence of each instrument in the rhythmic counterpoint, where constant changes of subdivision and varying pulses make the exact displacement of notes consistently complex. The music is not virtuosic in nature but rhythmically it is infinitely subtle. It is this constant flexibility of pulse which the conductor has to distil in the gestural language. In turn, this has to be conveyed to the performers with clarity and expression. This brings us to the broader issues of metronome marks.

The author is among many composers who are explicit in their tempo indications, the music being conceived at a specific tempo. In other words, the specified tempo is essential to the effectiveness of a musical idea. Why this is not the case with Boulez is a matter for conjecture. His own recordings testify to his preferences. For each individual conductor the assertion of subjective artistry is just as important here as it is in performing Bach or Brahms. So it is with Boulez. My own preference is to use the metronome marks of the 1957 edition, which seem to me to capture the aesthetic qualities of each movement.

Among Boulez's works *Le Marteau sans maître* is not exceptional in
tempo adjustments. For instance, in the 1990 recording of *Figures –
Doubles – Prismes* (Boulez with the BBC Symphony Orchestra) the
central section is considerably slower than the metronome mark
in the score. Other composers demonstrate a similar ambivalence.
Stravinsky's recordings of his own music vary quite considerably.
Schoenberg's markings are sometimes excessive in speed, and can blur
the refinements of a work such as the *Kammersymphonie*, to the point
where detail and expression are lost. Mahler shows even less concern by
avoiding metronome marks altogether. He preferred to leave decisions
of tempo to the performers. Where there is doubt, the main issue for a
conductor is to convey how the music resonates in his/her own artistic
sensibility to the pacing of a piece. Distilling the spirit of the music and
balancing the composer's indications with one's own subjective response
to the substance is the prime objective.

Beyond this we have issues of style, temperament, character, manner ...
but without a metronome mark these issues will never resolve variable
opinions about how a work should be paced. In spite of explicit markings
of characterisation, Sibelius avoids metronome marks and leaves a great
deal to conjecture with regard to tempo. I consider that Karajan seems
to misunderstand him by interpreting the passionate intensity of the
music with plodding pomposity and dragging tempi. Certainly, Karajan
did not lack a vibrant personality, which is such an important ingredient
in a conductor's role. Without it the pacing of a performance will always
sound wrong because orchestral musicians cannot coalesce in their
response to impassive direction. The primary prerequisite in performing
Le Marteau sans maître is pacing and realising the *expressive* character of
the often intensely flexible tempi.

Irregular pulse is discussed on pp. 22–43 in relation to *Le Sacre du printemps* and Rosbaud's graphic symbols identifying the two main variants. Boulez adds a further four configurations to them. This results in six in relation to one of the many time-signatures used.

Numbers 1–3 represent units related to a *single* beat.

1 | = half of a unit, sometimes used as a one-crotchet unit.

2 ⊓ = one unit involving a subdivided motif.

3 △ = one unit involving three subdivisions in a motif.

Numbers 4–6 represent single pulse units, but requiring a subdivision gesture from the conductor. Boulez uses an open-handed forward thrust for the subdivision (DVD track 2).

4 △ or △ = one unit with an additional subdivision of the first or last component of the unit, punctuated by a gesture.

5 △ = one compound unit subdivided symmetrically.

6 ⊔ = a subdivided compound unit where the second and third divisions contain a further compound motif in the music.

The variable height of the beat for each unit as discussed on p. 23 is imperative as a basis for directing every movement of this work. The subdivision of a compound unit is common in Boulez's own technique, where an open-handed forward thrust is used, rather than a downward beat. This secures a clear articulation of the subdivision of the unit in a motif. While this is always effective in Boulez's conducting, it is not absolutely necessary. My own view is that, pending on the speed of the pulse, it can be too fast a gesture for the players to respond to. This observation is based on the composer's own recommendation that all the conducting symbols included in the score are helpful suggestions, not rigorous requirements.

Throughout the work the technical clarity of gesture in conveying the irregular pulse patterns in most of the movements must sustain a quite virtuosic fluency. A central focus for the direction is imperative. Complete freedom from muscular tension is imperative. The lateral movement

of the wrist in conveying the geometric shapes of the beat is imperative.
The slightly angular fall of the downbeat in the opposite direction of the
subsequent beat is imperative. Without all of these components tension
will arise and rhythmic security and gestural clarity will be lost. DVD
track 2 illustrates the issue with the pulse units shown in Example 42.

EXAMPLE 42 Exercise in irregular time-units

Each of the bars has a different time-signature which establishes the
semiquaver quality of each unit. The number of beats in each bar differs,
so that the downbeat direction of bar 1 will be to the right, bar 2 to the
left, bars 3 and 4 straight down and bar 5 to the right. At a fast tempo the
variable height and swing between the △ and the ⊓ is just as important
as it is in *Le Sacre du printemps,* but the upbeat movement which controls
this factor will be done mainly with a wrist action supported by a slight
movement of the forearm, thinking of the elbow as the axis for any
arm movement. Once these fundamental characteristics become an
automatic muscular action, preparation for rehearsal and performance
can commence.

1 *Avant 'L'Artisanat furieux'*

DVD track 3, bars 1–20/42–52

The movement commences with the deployment of 'open boxes' and 'triangles'. Bars are accompanied by conventional time-signatures, but the number of beats is qualified by an integer. So that bar 17, while retaining a 2/4 status has the triplet figuration conducted in three. The pulse is essentially strict at this point, so the 3/8 in bar 18 must be exact as well. Therefore, it is essential to practise beating the triplet against a regular crotchet but making the two beats in bar 18 very fast. The basic pulse must be retained in the mind to make these rhythmic disruptions work. I find that instrumentalists respond more easily to a single triangle beat in bar 18. It is very important to control these beats with the varying heights for each value and that they become automatic in execution. The instrumentalists will find it quite easy if the displacement of the following beat is always anticipated by the associated height of its precedent.

Bars 21–4 are extremely difficult for the viola player. It is best to allow the player to lead with a more relaxed pace if necessary, and for the conductor to temporarily adapt to it. Make sure that the downbeat in bar 24 lifts at the correct height to reset the original tempo. Bar 33 involves a Boulez forward thrust. In my own experience it is clearer to make $\mid \sqcap$ into $\triangle$. It is always important to trust performers' ability to subdivide a figuration accurately, no matter how complex the contrapuntal texture. The important function for the conductor is to devise a technique which instils his/her own rhythmic perceptions in the players so that it becomes a mutual trust of accuracy. In this way a confident performance will result rather than a cautious one. In a complex work such as this it is vitally important to use exactly the same choreography in all rehearsals as in the performance, just as a dancer will prepare a consistent choreography. In this way the players will develop the essential trust which the conductor must generate in the arduous process of rehearsing this work to performance standard. Every nuance of rhythm, phrasing, dynamics and expression must be absolute in the conductor's perception and demonstrated in the consistency of the gestural patterns. I am aware of one conductor who only rehearsed

the first two movements of a Tchaikovsky symphony on the day of
the performance. When he failed to turn up for the second half of the
rehearsal the musicians simply practised their parts! This might work in
Tchaikovsky, but not in the repertoire discussed in this book.

The variable angles of the downbeat discussed earlier are absolutely
essential throughout the work. The consistency of the preparatory
beat and the downbeat is an extremely important focus for the players,
who are dealing with extremely concentrated material. The clarity
and consistency, especially the centralised focus of the downbeat, is
enormously helpful to them in seeing a constant assurance above their
music stands. This is especially important in places such as bar 37:
3 △⊓△. The differing values in bars such as 53, 54 and 55, in which
the basic pulse is constant, but the articulated units are all affected by
irrational figurations, shows Boulez recommending the first bar to
be conducted in two, which enhances the accentuated quintuplet. In
practising privately it is good to digest the speed of these notes by beating
three at ♩ = 168 and to articulate five verbally against it. Then conduct
the quintuplet in five and articulate three against that. This will also
secure the tempo of the following two bars. It is this kind of technical
exercise which develops into automatic control, just as two against three
does in Brahms. This will also resolve the issues in bars 61, 64, 67, 86
and 95. The gestural language of all the movements must be practised
and thoroughly learned to the point where it becomes automatic – not
unlike securing the fingering when learning a Rachmaninov étude. It is
just as imperative in *Le Marteau sans maître* because in rehearsal all of
a conductor's attention must be focused on the players and their needs
with an impeccable and consistent direction.

With a work as rhythmically complex as this, placing notes correctly in
the counterpoint can override the equally important aspect of detail in the
articulation, dynamic contrasts, phrasing and expression, the latter word
being one which Boulez does not avoid. The intensity of the music is lost
without an expressive projection of each phrase. These details cannot
be implemented by gesture, except in phrases which are in rhythmic
unison; but they must be *felt* by the conductor. In acknowledging the
work as a masterpiece, Stravinsky made the proviso that he could only
concentrate on two lines at a time. I find this puzzling, because it is

the textural composite of all the lines and their intensive detail which creates the exotic character of the music in such amazing mosaic colours. While Boulez is one of the composers who designed the mechanics of serialism, it is often overlooked that the density of detail in the expressive element of *Le Marteau sans maître* is a direct result of the integration of dynamics, duration, articulation and expression in the mechanics itself that is translated into the poetic beauty of so much of the work. Much has been made of the chosen instruments and their relationship to the needs of Char's poetry, but it is the mode of composition, where technique and imagination serve each other, that distinguishes the work as the masterpiece acclaimed by Stravinsky.

□ □ □ □

2 Commentaire I de 'Bourreaux de solitude'

DVD track 4, bars 54–64/103–14

Pierre Boulez,
Le Marteau
sans maître

Each of the movements contains distinctive graphic characteristics which illustrate their character, to some extent. Nos. 2 and 4 are the closest of the movements to mechanistic serialism, with single dynamics attached to each note. They are also distinguished by a unique graphic element. Many figurations are written with single horizontal ligatures representing quaver values with individual quaver or semiquaver ligatures allocated to each note as separate stems, as in bars 24–6.

The dual qualification emphasises the serial basis of the movements but complicates reading comprehension for the players, especially when the horizontal ligature spans across two units by a semiquaver. But the theoretic logic behind the graphics is valuable as a focus for the relationship of individual notes in phrasing the rhythmic motifs.

Boulez underlines the importance of the flute line being an articulated *legato*, in contrast to the xylophone, percussion and *pizzicato* viola – dry articulations, but all instruments being equally balanced in the texture. The complex rhythmic counterpoint which this creates is enhanced by each note being given an individual dynamic. With the rigorous tempo instructed by the composer, a rich tapestry of colourful punctuated texture emerges. It is very important for the players to be aware of these relationships. Their imaginative response to the concept is vital if a sea of notes without expression is to be avoided. Boulez recommends that the movement be conducted in quavers for the first two bars to establish the tempo, then in crotchets, returning to quavers when necessary (i.e. in bars which have semiquaver time-signatures). Because of the fairly steady tempo prescribed, my own approach is to sustain the quaver as the basic pulse unit until bar 56. This helps to achieve the *'ponctuellement'* nature of the nuances which Boulez specifies. It also assists the players to respond easily to quaver and semiquaver time-signatures as they arise.

On a theoretical level the notation is appropriate. On a practical level, in the individual parts rather than the score, conventional notation achieves a quicker and more immediately effective result. When I first directed the work, the violist, David Takeno, wrote out movements 2 and 4 in conventional notation and produced an impeccable performance very quickly. The other players involved followed his example with the same speedy results. For the conductor it cannot be emphasised sufficiently that the exact semiquaver relationships in bars such as 52–3 must demonstrate firm correspondence of well-practised subdivisions and with the appropriate height adjustment of each beat. It must look as easy and natural as possible.

Bar 54 signals this '*Rapide*' section as irregular, with an abrupt contrast. Here Boulez does not want a dynamic equality. The xylophone and viola (now *senza sord.*) should not be a balanced sonority, but distinctive against the now heavier sound of the percussion. Boulez notates a gradual accelerando through the first two bars. Bar 54 has a one beat triangle followed by a three beat triangle. Bar 55 has two irregular beats, but all three bars are pursuing a gradual *accelerando* to ♩ = 96.

My own preference is to subdivide the 5/8 to secure exact rhythmic punctuation throughout the *accelerando*, settling into crotchets in bar 56. The pause in bar 59 should be a simple roll of the hand at the base of the beat on the subdivision of the second beat. This will make it possible to simply raise the arm in preparation for the third beat, giving the players exact rhythmic preparation for the anacrusis. The lift after this third beat must be quicker than before to accommodate the faster tempo. The opening of the hand with the roll is a consistent characteristic of Boulez's own technique. Beating three in bar 85 also accommodates the *rallentando* and the pause. This is equally appropriate in bar 97. This characteristic becomes constant in the fourth movement and will be discussed in greater detail there. To sustain the intensity of articulation from bar 65 I have found that beating ♪ = 196 with a stable arm and only wrist action, works securely. This also makes it possible to provide the quaver anacrusis for bar 69, when the basic crotchet unit will accommodate the faster tempo.

The contrasts of fast and slow sections in this movement must be reflected in the exact application of the metronome marks. The metric contrasts and the textural balances are essential to the intensity of the coda (bar 103) when the flute rejoins the ensemble. This must be in five to accommodate the '*céder*' accompanying the flute's cadenza-like opening. It is important to keep bar 104 faster than the established tempo of ♪ = 120 in bar 105. My own preference is to subdivide at Boulez's

metronome mark of ♪ = 120 so that the sudden emphatic statement in
bar 111 can capture the statement of the xylophone triplets in the first
beat, which is a dominant statement of the inversion in the vibraphone's
opening figuration of the first movement. This phrase could be described
as a principal motif throughout the whole work.

There is another feature which concerns the complete work. At
the time of its composition, vibraphone and xylophone instruments
were played with two mallets, as stated earlier. Four mallets are now a
fundamental part of technique for these instruments. This is especially
valuable in the performance of rapid sections and widely spaced intervals,
giving much more articulative virtuosity to the character of the music.
Boulez and Roger Norrington were once featured in a television broadcast
in verbal combat over the relevance of authentic instruments being
deployed in present-day performances of early music. Boulez defended
his position by explaining that today he would not expect a percussionist
to use two mallets in *Le Marteau sans maître* simply because that was
the only available resource originally. I think this point of view could
be extended to the character of the alto flute, which, unlike today, was
rather weak in the top register when Boulez composed the work. The
opening *ossia* for the instrument in the very first bar of the whole work
demonstrates that Boulez was aware of this. Today such an *ossia* is
unnecessary.

A practical point might be useful in a live performance as opposed to a
recording. If a performer has an awkward turn in the part, the conductor
should be aware of it, in case a nominal pause might save a disaster. This
is the case in bars 74–5.

☐ ☐ ☐ ☐

3 *L'Artisanat furieux*

DVD track 5

No. 3 introduces the voice. Boulez composed this before the other movements in which the flute presents the prime series in bars 9–14. 'Der kranke Mond' from Schoenberg's *Pierrot Lunaire* was a strong motivation for the combination of flute and voice, which Boulez explains in a vivid discussion of the relationship between the two works in his *Orientations*.[10] This is essential reading for any conductor if the 'exotic' character of the music is to be realised. The marking '*Modéré sans rigueur*' is underlined with quite complex relationships between the metronome marks and the time-signatures. Following these explicit instructions in rehearsals the flautist can then be left to play these bars unconducted. The intensely expressive phrasing can then realise the improvisatory character of the music. I also consider that the visual aspect of absolute stillness on the platform enhances the beauty of a concentrated focus on the flautist. In spite of the complex time-signatures there is always an innate *pulse* in all of the movements, especially in no. 3. The need to sense the crotchet triplets in bar 3 in relation to the dynamic and articulation detail is essential to the expression of the phrase, just as it is in Debussy's *Syrinx*. At bar 5 the conductor must enter with the designated pulse, if irregular, in bar 6.

While direction needs to be discreet in this movement the contrasting characterisations must be conveyed in the gestures. The slow flexibility is best achieved with flowing arch-shapes and with constant attention to the principle of the upward flow becoming slower towards the top of the beat, as discussed in Part One (p. 17). A floating, relaxed arm is essential for the expression to be conveyed. Note that Boulez makes a distinction between melodic grace notes and *acciacature*. The former are written, and should be performed as semiquaver melodic inflections, while the latter should be crushed. This is consistent with the opening bassoon solo of *Le Sacre du printemps,* differentiations which are not observed in many performances. In passages such as bars 9–15 ghosting the beat, rather than punctuating it, is helpful to the performers, who need flexibility, but also motivic pulse in shaping the phrases. The slightly complex notation informs this aspect of interpretation. Once the main pulse of ♩ = 84 is established in bar 25, the pulse is less flexible, so that the motivic lines can be strongly characterised. Boulez suggests a subsidiary beat for the melodic grace notes in the flute part in bar 32.

In rehearsing a work which is not diatonic there are broad issues to consider in relation to music education. While there are outstanding performers who have studied non-diatonic music during their student days, there are many who have not. For the latter the standard tonal repertoire is the only foundation they have for their techniques. When faced with a modern or new work which requires non-tonal intervallic substance their traditional techniques do not provide them with the resources required for facility in execution, because the vocabulary is unfamiliar. If this seems like a criticism of teachers who fail to provide tuition in this repertoire, my only comment is that we are living in the twenty-first century. This does not mean to say that performers who have not had experience in learning a work such as *Le Marteau sans maître* cannot apply themselves to the task. It simply means that they will need advice and help from the conductor. This is especially so with singers, who have a far more difficult role without the use of fingers to displace sometimes complex intervallic phrases. No. 3 is full of wide intervals which do not have a tonal centre. The flute part is written in G, so the extra consideration of transposing the part adds to the challenges for the singer. An experienced singer will work out cue notations and simply practise with muscular memory for pitching, which serves them in all circumstances. For the inexperienced it is up to the conductor to instruct with a piano in the learning process. Taking groups of two to three notes at a time, play them as a chord so that the singer will perceive them as such when vocalising. Later, join the last and first notes of consecutive chords, so that links in the phrases can also be digested. With repetition and the help of keyboard monitoring, muscular memory and aural perception will soon take over. Then the details of expression and rhythmic association can be founded on pitch security. It is very important to underline the importance of choreographic consistency from the conductor at the very outset and throughout the work during the rehearsal process. So learn to play the vocal part with the left hand and conduct with the right for each movement during *répétiteur* sessions with the singer. I should add that I have been lucky enough to have performed the work with singers such as Jane Manning and Alison Wells, who needed absolutely no coaching. These superb singers have set a brilliant example of artistic commitment to living composers that is incomparable.

☐ ☐ ☐ ☐

4 Commentaire II de 'Bourreaux de solitude'

DVD track 6

Boulez asks for pauses (⌒) and stopping points (⊓) to be abrupt interruptions in the tempo, except where indicated to the contrary. In relation to the idiosyncratic notation, this requires considerable technical resource from the conductor. Bar 4 serves as an example. The pause on the first semiquaver is followed by a motif on the second. The only way to secure exact rhythmic precision for this entry is to give a second downbeat, which, of course, is not articulated by the performers. It will be noted that the first semiquaver contains a *laissez vibrer* symbol. The second downbeat will act as a cut-off for this (as if a semiquaver rest) and the performers can play securely on the second semiquaver entry. The 'stop' symbol (⊓) across the following bar line is accompanied by the abbreviation 'ét', signifying ' *étouffer*', to damp. These distinguishing indications are consistent throughout the movement and must be strictly observed. The instruction accompanying these signs states that the pauses should be extremely varied from short to long; the stopping points should be brief and uniform. Both signs have the variable qualifications stated above, with an occasional *tenuto* instruction added. The varying tempo marks and metronome marks also provide an indication of the quality of a pause.

The horizontal ligatures with individual note values attached to each note have been mentioned (p. 157). Boulez states that these joining ligatures in the xylophone and viola pizzicato are placed to avoid too brutal an attack, which is not required at these places. Elsewhere he explains that the textural palate of each movement is established on 'a chain linking each instrument to the next by a feature common to both: voice–flute, breath; flute–viola, monody; viola–guitar, plucked strings; guitar–vibraphone, long resonance; vibraphone–xylophone, struck bars of metal or wood'.[11] With this palette in mind, the conductor must establish the sonic colour for every moment in the work to achieve an effective application of the musical brush. This is a good metaphor to keep in mind while determining the gestural language required for the textural mobility of each movement. The special characteristics in no. 4 are innate to Boulez's conducting technique and style. The very first bar requires a gesture that will inform each pause, whether short or long: preparation and an assertive fall to the base, followed by a small loop to the right, finishing with a plateau gesture, throwing the hand open, but not with splayed fingers (DVD track 2). At double downbeat pauses the preparation of the second beat will establish the tempo of the ensuing phrase.

Bars 4–5 expose a further characteristic of the movement: constant fluctuations of tempi and metronome marks. In music which requires exact horizontal location between all the parts in intricate rhythmic counterpoint this is not easy to achieve. It is where the loop action takes on a second function. Following the first downbeat on the pause, the second downbeat will establish the basic pulse up to the second crotchet beat. In order to secure the *accelerando* the loop should subdivide on the percussion semiquaver at a faster pace. A slower tempo must be established by the preparation for bar 5, which has a *ritardando* on the second beat. The subdivision loop should be made on the third subdivision of the second beat with a slightly lazier action. These two kinds of pause-control form the basis for the whole movement, especially in creating the immediate impact of a sudden fast rush of tempo in places such as bars 9 and 36.

When a semiquaver anacrusis has to be accommodated after a pause (bars 14–15), following the pause loop, simply lift the preparation for bar 15 (no click!) so that the downbeat is anticipated by the vibraphone and viola in placing the final semiquaver of bar 14. It is very easy to become over-protective in controlling such moments. Apparent simplicity is the rule. No gesture should involve tension of any kind. The more natural the movement appears, the more assured will be the response.

Boulez does not include subdivision beats in bars 15, 25, 26, 30–3, 46 and 49–51. I recommend beating quavers in all of them, especially when varying tempi occur. This helps to control the rhythmic counterpoint and any fluctuations of pulse required. Two-part counterpoints in one instrument are usually controlled by dynamic differences between the two 'voices': e.g. guitar in bars 25 and 27; vibraphone in bars 11 and 15; viola in bars 43 and 49; xylophone in bars 50 and 55. The separate 'voices' are written with the conventional upward and downward stems. It is important that the dynamic differences are exaggerated. As in no. 2, the effectiveness of distinctive dynamics should be a prime objective in initial rehearsals. No live performer could possibly grade the levels to mechanical exactness, nor is it desirable to do so. The important issue is to have a constant field of articulations which make each part independent in projection, but creating a 'mirror ball' of splintered sounds. If this is sustained up to the pause in bar 63, the surprise of a constant dynamic in each part at bar 64, punctuated by the *cloche double*, is very powerful.

With such complexities in rehearsal and performance it is wise to use a sign to indicate where the double downbeats occur. I use a colour-coding for this element: green spectacles! Tempo gradations and pauses are in red. I also mark the *accelerandi* and *ritardandi* with rising and falling red arrows respectively. (These are my own colour preferences which can be personalised in alternative colours if necessary.) It is also wise to mark the turns in parts at bars 38, 46 and 90. With all of these cautionary measures the choreography will remain secure and the conductor's attention can be focused entirely on rehearsal points together with an aural perception concentrated on achieving the composer's vision.

5 *Bel édifice et les pressentiments, version première*

DVD track 7

Of all the movements this is the most complex to conduct. Within sixteen bars there are twelve metronome indications. As with all the movements they are in parentheses but qualified by an initial tempo indication with three variables: ♩ = ca. 56↙80↗108. The reason for such variety is clarified by the statement: '*Tempo et nuances très instables*'. '*Assez vif*' describes the characterisation, then there is a further instruction immediately prescribing '*presser*'. Boulez also explains that the tempi are indicated in relation to the main metronome mark of 80. On each side of this the metronome mark should be extreme. All of this has to take into account the extremely difficult viola part in this opening section. Again, the difference between crushed grace notes and melodic embellishments must be maintained. This is emphasised in the vocal line in bar 16 when Boulez asks for '*La petite note très courte*'. From a purely practical point of view this is important in a bar such as 11. In the second beat the initial grace notes need to be played early in the semiquaver rest in order to complete the quintuplet figuration with the prescribed accelerando ('*revenir au Tempo*'). It is imperative that the conductor's beat sustains a flowing character with a clear anticipation of the downbeat, so that the player can accommodate the quite complex phrase rhythmically, to land on the trill forcefully but elegantly.

The tempo changes should be regulated by the varying height of the beat so that the players can *anticipate* where the variable beat of the pulse will land. In this way the players can accommodate the notes within a motif comfortably, as long as the conductor senses the actual performance of each phrase. This is the same principle that an accompanist adopts in leading and not following a soloist. Further complexities arise from the numerous *accelerandi* and *rallentandi* within the phrases. Control of this extreme flexibility of pulse is dependent on the varying height and natural fall of the arm as discussed in Part One. Because of this, decisions on choreography should be part of the process of learning the score by the conductor. In relation to this movement such a process is imperative. The subdivision of a bar in one rehearsal but not in another is very confusing for the players. My own plan is as follows:

Bars 1–6   As Boulez prescribes

Bars 8–9   In four. This provides security for the triplets in the
    guitar and viola parts, especially important during the advance
    in tempo towards bar 10, which is in two.

Bars 11–12 In two, to allow the flexibility required for the viola, as
    discussed above.

Bars 13–14 In three.

Bars 15–18 As Boulez prescribes. In bar 15 the singer requires lots
    of space for the quintuplet; hence the short break over the bar
    line. Following this, simply 'ghost' the beat until the flute entry
    in bar 18.

Bars 19–20 The unison chords for all the instruments must
    be precise. Beating each articulation rather than the time-
    signature makes this three in bar 19 and four in bar 20, giving
    absolute control of the '*ralentir*' and uniform *diminuendo*.

Bars 21–9   As Boulez prescribes. In *rallentandi* the fall of the
    arm will be slower (but still advancing in speed) and in the
    accelerandi the lift of the arm will be faster.

Bar 30   Give one crotchet beat for the singer to float the
    quintuplet towards the break, giving the conductor a clear
    preparation for the third, fourth and fifth quaver beats in the
    new, *subito tempo*.

Bars 31–9   As Boulez prescribes.

Bars 40–3   I recommend one beat to a bar throughout, so that the
    flute and viola can measure their irrational note groups with
    absolute precision, helped by the conductor's clear anticipation
    of where the beats will land at all points of the '*presser*' section.
    This also provides quite a dramatic fall into the silence of the
    first beat of bar 43 with the composer's recommendation of
    crotchet beats.

Bar 47   Boulez recommends three. I prefer one followed by
    a 'loop' pause to allow the viola enough freedom to measure
    the septuplet. There is a player's page turn at this point which
    should be considered.

Bars 48–62   As Boulez prescribes. It should be noted that the open boxes and triangles must be distinguished from the quaver units indicated for the conductor in bars such as 55, which is in three, and 60–1, which are in four. For the singer's anacrusis in bar 62 simply lift the arm away from the pause (see Part One on preparatory beats) so that she can place her phrase in relation to where the downbeat will fall. In bar 63 I prefer ⊓ △ beats to secure unison articulation.

Bars 64–9   Because of the many unison motifs, I find three in a bar sustains the gradual intensity towards bar 69 effectively. At bar 70 △⊓ (in two) is helpful to the unison groups in the flute and viola.

Bars 72–5   Again, for rhythmic accuracy I prefer two beats to a bar, but three in bar 74 to accommodate the *rallentando*.

Bars 76–7   In quavers, for the same reason. Then as Boulez prescribes up to bar 96.

Bar 97   The important triplet motif thrown between the guitar and viola (*pizzicato*) in a '*presser*' pulse is emphasised by four in a bar.

Bar 99   Boulez subdivides the three-quaver unit into a crotchet and quaver pattern. My own preference is to beat the whole bar in five, driving into crotchets in bar 100.

Bar 104   Safer in four to accommodate the sudden tempo change on the third quaver. This necessitates three in bar 105 to sustain a change to three crotchets in bar 106 (getting faster).

Bar 109   Gives the viola freedom with only one beat and a gentle loop to accommodate the break.

The incredibly beautiful simplicity of the short coda at bar 110 should be approached with a sense of the profound nature of the poem at this point: 'Des yeux purs dans les bois cherchant en pleurant la tête habitable'. It is an example of what Boulez describes as René Char's 'concentrated expression'.[12] From ♩ = 60 the music fades to ♪ = 52 with the singer at an almost voiceless *ppp* at the close. The extraordinary contrast to the complexity of the rest of the music can be exaggerated without fear of offending the composer's declaration that 'no play is made with the ambiguities of an aesthetic situation'.[13] For the conductor and players to appear as motionless as possible in these final eight bars can add to the 'concentrated expression' of the words and the music. Stillness should remain through the long pause as indicated.

6 *Bourreaux de solitude*

As far as direction is concerned, no. 6 is comparatively straightforward, with all the instruments involved for the first time. This is an intense movement, but static in character. Each instrumental line contains no motivic material, each note being placed as a precious stone in the ensemble setting. The sustained character of each individual line should exaggerate the constant dynamic changes and articulated nuances to achieve the kaleidoscopic nature of the resulting textural complex. Because the metronome mark is slow ($\goodbreak$ = 56) the pulse for beating is on the cusp between subdivision and main metre, especially in compound bars such as bar 25. The footnote at the opening underlines this sense of dichotomy. Boulez instructs the conductor to beat quavers during the first two measures to stabilise the movement, then to beat crotchets. He leaves a great deal to the conductor's judgement by suggesting a return to a quaver beat whenever it is necessary. There is a sense here that the bar lines should not dictate pulse. This is emphasised by the fact that the very gentle maracas ('*sempre-sans nuances*') are never articulated in unison with another instrument until bar 52. This sense of suspended animation must inform the decisions made. Bar 25 does pose a question. The time-signature is 6/8 with ♩ = 56. Boulez's conducting signs indicate two beats in the bar, which would result in a tempo of ♩. = 37.3, which is, of course, too slow to achieve security in the counterpoint and too unorthodox to be valid. So six it is! A return to crotchets in bar 26 is essential for the floating character of the music. It is especially important in this movement to exaggerate the differentiation of dynamics in individual instruments. When performing Beethoven it is easier for the players to listen to each others' parts to locate the involvement of their own. It is more difficult to achieve the required balance in this kind of work. This is a rather strange recommendation to make but, initially it is useful to ask the players *not* to listen to other parts, but to concentrate on the constant dynamic changes in their own parts. As rehearsals progress and familiarity grows stronger, the listening process will develop as long as the conductor has instructed such an approach. In spite of the mosaic texture of this movement, linear characteristics are important, especially at the climactic section for the flute in bars 75–8.

A double downbeat is recommended at bar 91. I have found that beating quavers from here to the close keeps the rather splintered substance in clear rhythmic counterpoint.

Pierre Boulez,
Le Marteau
sans maître

DVD track 8

In sharp contrast this is a rapid, virtuosic display for flute, vibraphone and guitar. As in no. 5, there is a constant fluctuation of pulse. There are not so many changes of metronome mark, but there are only nine (mostly isolated) bars which remain at a constant pulse. I have found it especially useful in rehearsals of this movement to mark ascending and falling arrows above the *accelerandi* and *rallentandi* indications in the score. This helps to give absolute aural concentration to the players and to sustain consistency in the variable tempi. Boulez uses the word '*cédez*' sometimes to indicate that at such points the conductor must yield before sensing the speed of an ensuing *accelerando*. The rests and short pauses should be controlled with the loop and extended hand gesture. When the speed reaches ♩ = 208 in bar 17 the quintuplet must be conducted in two, as Boulez suggests, but gestures must be made only with a hand and forearm action because of the speed. Applying the basic gesture of the downbeat in 2/4 veering to the right, the upbeat must be higher for the △ than the crotchets in the following bar, which have to be simply a right swing, returning with a loop and extended hand for the pause. At bar 28 note the turn required in one of the parts. From bar 39 to the close it is useful to practise privately the gradual dying of the movement with the following points in mind.

When the *ritardando* begins in bar 41, each bar retains a similar speed for each quaver so that the figurations belie the fact that they appear to be faster in the actual graphics. This is important when calculating the height of the first duple beat of bar 43, which should be the same as the quintuplet triplet beat in the previous bar. By bar 44 the pulse of one beat to a bar is temporarily settled. The '*Tempo sub.*' (♩ = 168) on the third quaver is a surprise which requires the upward swing after the downbeat in bar 45 to be very rapid, but immediately slow for the subsequent dying away in the guitar, each downbeat being slightly higher in each bar. Note that the last *pp* note for the guitar has a *laissez vibrer* tie, accompanied by the 'very short pause' instruction, so that no. 8 will follow abruptly.

□ □ □ □

DVD track 9

This begins deceptively with a regular quaver pulse. While the score indicates open box and triangle recommendations, the metronome mark of ♪ = 152 paradoxically implies a quaver beat. This is certainly favoured by the percussionists I have worked with. The gradual *accelerando* finishes at an only marginally faster tempo of ♪ = 184 in bar 20, where the *accelerando* and clattering articulations of the vibraphone and xylophone leave the *pp* flute sustained through the pause. Again, the preparation for the following slow section should simply be a raised arm action in the new tempo to allow the flute to place the anacrusic grace-note figuration in measured anticipation of the downbeat. Bar 21 involves a characteristic common to bars 25, 28, 32, 45, 75, in which the flute has rhapsodic solos which interrupt the main pulse. There is very little activity from other instruments at these moments, but displacement of notes must be consistently measured. Here, the conductor must remain discreet but punctilious in accommodating the flautist's diversions, which, in bars 28 and 32, the marking '*à l'aise*' is vital to the musical expression. In bar 21 the conducting symbols must be observed explicitly.

The quaver pause on the second beat should simply stop at the base without any other gesture. This makes it possible to make the simple upward preparation for the subdivision, essential to the percussionist. Beating quavers in bar 25 provides ensemble security as long as the fourth and fifth beats move forward rapidly to emphasise the regular crotchet tempo of bar 26. Bar 28 benefits from quaver beats in a similar way. The △ symbols in bars 29 and 30 can be confusing for the players unless directed by Boulez himself. My own approach is not to put in subdivision detail unless it is the only way to achieve security, as in bars 32 and 33, where a quaver beat can achieve firm rhythmic assurance, especially in bar 33. On the basis of this approach I recommend quavers in bars 36, 39, 40, 41 and 45. The accumulating intensity of bars 47–50 acts as a coda to this opening section.

In contrast to the opening section bars 51–66 sustain a consistent tempo in which the 5/8 bars react well to quaver beats, as opposed to crotchets elsewhere. When the downbeat short pause is reached at bar 67, it is best to adopt the double downbeat principle, especially in relation to the new, slower tempo. The subdivision recommended previously applies up to bar 80, especially in bars 76–80.

Bars 81–92 represent the most radical revision of tempo between the first and second editions. In the first the metronome mark is ♪ = 126 throughout the whole section. The vibraphone and xylophone parts are impossible to play at this speed. The second edition gives a more practical indication of tempo by reducing it to ♪ = 88 (underlined) with margins of ♪ = 104 and 76 on either side. This is a great relief to the players! In both editions Boulez qualifies the pacing with '*très librement*'. Even with the four-mallet technique in modern performances, bars such as 87 and 91 achieve the virtuosic requirement only with a flexible, indeed *supple* 'ghosting' from the conductor. It is a section in which the players must lead the way and the conductor must be submissive. The instruction says that grace notes should not be played in a strict tempo but built (through their number and the tension of their intervals) on a tempo sufficiently fluent. It is important to add that they should be played as fast as possible and as soon *after* the previous main note as is necessary to articulate them all in time for the following main note. The vibraphone part in bar 87 illustrates this need on the third quaver beat, where the three-grace-note group should begin immediately after the G♯ of the main beat. The sensitivity of the conductor to the practical instrumental challenges of any score is important, but never more so than in this work.

With a marking of ♩ = 88 on the second beat of bar 93 the pulse does not change, but the quaver becomes a crotchet. Boulez marks a brisk *accelerando* in the first beat, subdividing to indicate the new character as well as the new relationships. There is a turn at bar 98, so that a notional pause might be considered in this rapid *ritardando* beat, settling into the gentle murmurings of each instrument, the bongos remaining *ppp* from bar 84 onwards. There is an optional extra quaver beat signalled in the score which must be left to individual preferences. The lift of the tempo back to ♩ = 88 is very important in order to achieve the sense of rhapsodic intrusion by the flute in bar 110. From bar 111, quaver beats help to control the path back to ♩ = 88 in bar 119.

Bars 123 to the close provide an example of Boulez's intense need for a sense of pulse in the motivic material, no matter how flexible the actual tempo. In the conducting symbols the quintuplet motifs in each crotchet unit are subdivided in two unequal beats: △⌐ or ⌐△. There are wide variations of tempo, but freedom is needed for the players to play the rhythmic structures without accentuation in the articulations, even when loud. My own experience dictates that the subdivisions which work well for Boulez's technique become too intrusive when I attempt them. The principle which I adopt is that, if the beat is designed to fall into the base-line and making the upward swing get slower towards the top, the anticipation of each beat by players will be comfortable, no matter how variable the pulse. This is an act of mutual faith between players and conductor. The conductor's pulse must not change from one rehearsal to another, so that the players can calculate their own subdivisions rhythmically and confidently within the fluctuating pulse, consistent in all rehearsals and performance. This is especially important in a place such as bar 124, where the flautist is required to play 'à l'aise'. To control the *ritardando* in the very slow bar 127 I find subdivision into six achieves accuracy and rhythmic precision. The *accelerando* in bar 128 can be achieved on the same basis, with three crotchet beats and players subdividing mentally. While bar 134 works well in six it is important to sense the constant dissolving character implicit in the score. Again, too many conducted subdivisions can spoil the effect of these subtle mallet strokes which prepare us for all the elements of the previous movements being drawn together in the ninth movement.

9 *Bel édifice et les pressentiments, double*

DVD track 10

The movement is punctuated by pauses and interruptions. It is very important to sense the architectural design behind the constant changes of texture and movement. The characterisation must be reflected in the conductor's gestural language in order to make every single note in the movement intensely meaningful in musical expression. Without such intensity, whether quiet and calm or loud and vibrant, the piece will sound short-winded and stop–start. There are no aspects of technique required by the conductor which have not been exposed in the other movements. The varying metronome marks must be seen in the light of growing or waning intensity.

The conducting symbols might seem contradictory at first sight. As explained in Part One (p. 25), the two basic units are ⊓ and △ for duple and triple single units to a beat. When the stems of the duple unit are spread wide apart they indicate two separate units but only one beat. This is apparent in bar 4 in which one crotchet and one dotted quaver units are implied – two beats in the bar. In bar 5 the symbols imply one crotchet beat, one quaver beat on the pause, followed by two quaver beats.

Bar 6 contains three quaver beats on single stems. The initial instruction '*Tempo libre de récit*' makes it clear what characterisation Boulez wishes to establish. There are more metronome marks in the second edition than in the first, which indicates that quite excessive flexibility is required, but under absolute control from the conductor. The addition of conducting symbols throughout the work in the second edition is not simply a technical resource but a form of graphics which tell the conductor almost as much about the music as the notes themselves. In other words, the conductor has been conceived by the composer in the process of composition as a performing element in the work and not someone who simply enters the arena to direct the operation at the performance stage. This is a major innovation in the graphic construct of a score, emphasising the mutual trust required between instrumentalists and conductor. The irregularity of the pulse in all of the movements, except no. 6, gives the conductor an intensely challenging responsibility in the need to evolve a subtle technique of

highly complex gestural language, while assimilating the expressive
and technical conditions for each instrumental part at all times in the
performance and rehearsals.

There are several places where the conducting symbols can be treated
with subjective interpretations. A few illustrations will explain the issue:
bar 17 is more secure in four; bar 18 is clearly best as written; bar 19
shows a contradiction between the rhythmic grouping of two dotted
quavers and the 3/8 time-signature and symbols. I prefer to make this
a 6/8 bar in two, which also helps to settle the indicated two beats in
bar 20. The apparent contradiction between the symbols in bars 18 and
29 (at a similar speed) is simply an indication that there are few absolutes
in the quest for expressive nuances in conducting techniques.

Bar 42 can benefit security by being beaten in six, then quavers right
up to bar 47, then crotchet beats up to bar 50. The manner in which
Messiaen distinguishes between semiquaver and quaver subdivisions of
the unit is not observed by Boulez in bars 57–9. Using the same symbols
for successive bars in 6/16 and 6/8 is not consistent with the Messiaen
principle, but less fussy, especially as the 6/8 is more secure in quavers
at ♪ = 120. Bar 67 introduces a new subdivision of the triangle: △

This indicates that the triplet beat should be divided evenly as two
dotted quavers. Instrumentalists respond well if the variable height
principle for ⊓ and △ is adopted without the suggested subdivision
of the triangle, which can enhance the explosive entry of the whole
ensemble in bar 68 and for the ensuing rhythmic unison chords. This
is especially important in bar 71 where the triangles are half the value of
those in bar 70, but not relative to the open box in the first beat. My own
way of dealing with this is to make the first beat into a four-semiquaver
box: □ relative to the three semiquaver triangles, virtually a metric
modulation between the two bars. Bar 72 is in strict crotchets. In bar 73
I simply give the first beat plus a forward thrust for the final semiquaver.
Similar situations occur in places such as bars 82–7. The most important
element of rhythmic clarity in the beat is to sustain consistent directional
geometry with an equally consistent differentiation of height in relation
to pulse and tempo relationships.

When the flute takes over from the singer it is appropriate to leave
it to the player, once rehearsed, in the tempo variants. The rest of the

movement poses no further technical issues until bars 125–31. After two beats in bar 125, keeping the second beat less high to accommodate the '*presser*' we find a new symbol: in 3/16 subdividing the main unit. With two bars of 1/4 + 1/16 through a *rallentando,* my own preference is to simplify the beat in each bar (including the +1/16) from bars 126–8. The anticipation of the downbeat is all that the percussionist needs to place the final anacrusis before the passionately exotic final section, with the percussion in dialogue with the flute. While these final moments travel an effectively improvisational path, the beating must be quite assertive in order to accommodate the sometimes frenetic activity of the percussionist in striking and damping the tam-tams and gong. There is a magic quality in each phrase. Like the earlier part of the movement, the phrases are short-lived and static. Framed by the percussion the flute contrasts rhapsodic arabesques with contemplative phrases. The sheer beauty of these final statements must be absolutely in the conductor's mind while indicating the undulating pulse, which, like the words, is at the centre, but absent.

□ □ □ □

Karlheinz Stockhausen, Zeitmaße

Score: Universal Edition (London), 1957

In the twenty-first century we are able to view the individual evolution of each composer who came through the Darmstadt experience as an historical record. While they all travelled the gauntlet of integral serialism they are by no means the product of a 'school' of composition. Each of them developed an entirely distinctive vocabulary and style which retained only the shadows of Darmstadt. When we consider the output of such strongly established composers and many others, the diversity of substance in their work is vast. Darmstadt was an important breeding ground for all of them, but subsequently they trod their own paths of development. Stockhausen and Boulez were close friends, but each recognised and respected the other's independence. 'No rivalry existed between us', Stockhausen said. 'Each of us has worked out his own way of life, there has always been collateral self-knowledge and mutual appreciation.'[14] Boulez's comments on the serial days of Darmstadt have been remarked on (p. 147).

Zeitmaße was composed in 1955–6. It represents for Stockhausen what *Le Marteau sans maître* meant to Boulez – a break with the dogmatism of serialism. A series *is* presented in bars 1–3, but presented in three-part counterpoint. Neither the note values nor the dynamics are serialised, as in integral serialism techniques. They are, in fact, quite conventional and expressive in gesture. This is an aspect common to the complete work and one which a conductor would be wise to consider.

In discussing the issues of pitch and time in his essay '... how time passes ...'[15] Stockhausen's explanations are rather convoluted and even questionable on acoustic matters. But in this composition the integration of both elements fosters a unique sound world. Early experiments in electronic generation of sound brought a recognition of sine waves as a combining factor of pitch and time. Very low frequencies can be heard as rhythmic pulses rather than audible pitches, whereas higher frequencies are heard as distinctive pitches. The title of the work indicates that it is an essay in tempo and pulse.

The performance directions make it clear that a conductor is not part of the concept. Five instructions identify the principal characteristics:

1 Exact observance of metronome marks.

2 Judging the speed of a fast section by the smallest note-value of
   a group.

3 Establishing the tempo of a passage by the breathing capacity of
   a player.

4 The ratio proportions of tempi in a passage by the rate of
   slowing-down to control irregularity of tempo.

5 Deciding the tempo by the value of a note at the end of a group.

These instructions end with a general comment about an 'approximate
control of measures' indicated in the score 'to proportionate scale'. All
of this means that individual instrumentalists are required to determine
the duration and expression of events according to the five performing
instructions. The amount of rehearsal time needed to respect these
requirements is disproportionate to the work's 12-minute place in a
programme. For this reason most subsequent performances have been
conducted. In sections where each performer pursues independent time
values in variable tempi, Stockhausen has been meticulous in drawing
the lines in the score to proportionate scale. This provides the conductor
with a clear indication of the vertical relationships which should result
in the performance, in spite of the required independence of each
performer.

There are many published references to the work, including
Stockhausen's own,[16] all of which present detailed analyses of the
structural principles of the work. The conductor must go a stage beyond
this. While the gestural language required to ensure the appropriate
displacement of notes is of prime concern, this alone will not bring
a performance to life in such a complex work. It is the expressive
characterisation of each part which makes the texture and counterpoint
work in the imaginative perception which Stockhausen describes as
'structures [which] move about between strictly regulated time-fields in
which varying numbers of notes are *pulverized into vibrating swarms of
sound*' (my italics).[17] This kind of image informs sections such as bars
29–40. In contrast, the phrase at bar 12 evokes a Tristanesque dynamic
folding of the phrase – warmth and beauty in each moment. This is soon
contradicted by a completely opposite characterisation from the flute

in bar 16 – an aggressive display which soon expires with a *rallentando* into silence, preparing the new tempo for the cor anglais to continue its previous expressive statement. Such contrasts require an exaggerated form of phrasing. Not unlike Berg in this respect, the details of phrasing (even a *staccato* dot over a *tenuto* symbol) are linked to the conglomerate textural variety which informs every bar of the piece. In the conventional wind quintet repertoire performances can be very dull if a wide range of contrasting dynamics are not observed. Details of dynamic variation are even more essential in *Zeitmaße*. A clarinet can play equally quietly at both extremes of register. Although there is an *ossia* in bar 87, the clarinet is required to play a phrase covering more than four octaves, from a low F to a top A, with a *diminuendo* to *piano* at the top of the phrase. Clarinettists are capable of performing such an event with expressive intensity. All of the other instruments are required to perform similar wide – ranging cascades in the same section. With a conductor involved such a moment can be full of varying shades and colours if details are strongly focused.

Another issue to consider is pulse. The contraction and rarefaction of note values in all the parts of bars 87–91 and similar sections must convey individual pulse associations in the motivic phrasing. Stockhausen specifies a consistent metronome mark for these bars, but each part contains figurations with irrational subdivisions of each unit. The values must be explicit within the regular pulse to achieve motivic variety. This is especially significant in the cor anglais part. While the whole phrase is governed by a *legato* line, there are explosive interruptions with accented notes and 'gestossen' (harsh, detached) figurations before the settling moment in bar 93.

The implications of the title go beyond the interpretation of the word as 'time', because it has implications of pulse. A motif or figuration cannot be effective without a pulse mechanism, no matter how irregular. This must be a strong element of interpretation for the players as well as for the conductor. In an unfamiliar idiom players can easily be bound up with the notes at the expense of expressive character. If a conductor simply beats time in a work like *Zeitmaße* the players will not be encouraged to project the aesthetic character of the music, so easy in Mozart but equally necessary in the more elusive Stockhausen.

In discussing the beating patterns and conducting gestures for the work, conventional measures, such as the first bars, need not occupy us. The terms *beschleunigen* and *verlangsamen* are always followed by metronome marks for following sections. Bar 2 is an example of the need to occasionally subdivide. The last beat has an *accelerando* which should be subdivided to establish the faster quaver beat in bar 3 in the manner of *Le Marteau sans maître* Stockhausen prescribes eight quaver beats in bar 5 but the character is achieved more fluently in four at $\bullet$ = 66. In bar 16 the flute benefits from a subdivision of the third and fourth beats in establishing the *rallentando* into a very slow crotchet in bar 17. The need for explicit durations of notes is stressed at bar 23 when players are instructed to make even the shortest notes (semiquavers) exact durations. Subdividing the fourth beat of bar 27 enhances the accelerando and secures the rhythmic unison of the following bar. Bar 29 introduces the first use of instruction 2, where the alternating instruments play 'as fast as possible' against strictly measured music in other instruments. While the conductor beats a steady pulse at $\bullet$ = 112 it is essential that he/she is aware of the paramount importance in rehearsal of Stockhausen's instruction to keep 'dynamics in equal proportion'. It is also important to cue the clarinet and cor anglais entries in bar 34. After they have completed the 'as fast as possible' measures the demarcation point can be elusive. The oboist would also benefit from being aware of the fifth beat entry of the cor anglais, so that the instruction to 'play in one breath' up to bar 44 will help him/her to survive. If Stockhausen had composed the work a decade later such an instruction would not have been required. Circular breathing is now a standard element of oboe technique. It is a valuable asset also in Bach *obbligati*, especially in *Jesu, Joy of Man's Desiring*. The requirement in all such sections throughout the work is that the time-signature element should be conducted strictly while cues for new entries must be provided for the players. In bar 39 this is especially important for the flautist, who has to rejoin the measured bars after a very rapid series of free grace-note cascades.

A demarcation indication is a useful device for any work which deploys free or improvisational elements against measured time-signatures. In relation to the section under discussion it is helpful to the players if mirror-beating is avoided in bars 29–41. The left hand should only be used for cues. Apart from the flute, all the other instruments need is a clear indication when bar 41 arrives. If the left hand remains mainly inactive throughout the section, bar 41 can be cued with both hands together, providing a uniform downbeat. Such a measure also saves rehearsal time if explained in advance. All that is needed from this point up to bar 75 is a strict beat, especially when the symbol requires the players to raise their instruments in a rapid gesture for accentuated effect. The rhythmic unison from bars 55–8 is a surprise moment. Controlling the varying tempi here can be done by applying the technique discussed on p. 42, keeping in mind that the variable speed of the upward swing provides clarity of pulse for the anticipated downbeat. Once the rhythmic structure has been secured in rehearsal the rapid succession of varied and individual dynamics in each part must be explicit to achieve the textural result which makes the idea work.

In bars 41–110 there are no decisive metronome marks. Bar 53 simply indicates a slower pulse. As with all works with constantly varying pulses, it is important for the conductor to establish an exact tempo to be replicated in every rehearsal. If there is any alteration from one rehearsal to another the players will be uneasy and time will be wasted. Creating one's own metronome speed at bar 53, where *langsamer* is all that is specified, will establish consistency in rehearsal and performance.

The low B for the flute at bar 67 was only attainable on a German instrument at the time of composition. In a performance which I conducted in 1965 the flautist, James Galway, used a cigar case to temporarily extend the tube of his instrument for this moment. It is no longer an issue in the twenty-first century, now that professional flautists generally use instruments with a low-B foot joint.

Bar 74 illustrates the function of the fifth instruction when the initial tempo is re-established by 'the shortest possible mensural unit at the end of the group'.

In controlling the *accelerando* the conductor establishes the '*langsamer*' tempo accelerating to a very rapid speed half-way through the fourth quaver beat of bar 76. Sustaining quaver beats in this bar is advisable. From bar 77 the *ritardando* can be free. But an abrupt 'so schnell wie möglich' can be achieved with a lateral rapid movement of the hand, using the wrist as axis. In bar 80 we have a suggested metronome mark of 'at least ♪ = 88', which I recommend as maximum. The reason for this is purely musical. In bar 82 there is a magic moment on the third and fourth beats, when all the instruments remain static on a chord spread over six octaves. Each part sustains differing dynamic inflections. If balanced well it creates a band-filtering effect, evoking the influence of the composer's experiments in the electronics studio. The rhythmic unison required after this chord must be impeccable. My recommendation for beating patterns in this section are as follows: the first three crotchet beats require no explanation, the third beat on the tie being a conventional springboard for the release of the following figurations; with the fourth beat (a quaver) a Boulezian plateau gesture will secure the semiquaver before the pause; the fifth quaver beat should be preceded by a double downbeat on the pause, for the players to use it as a quaver preparation for the unison entry; the fifth quaver follows at the same speed.

A stated tempo of 'at most ♪ = *ca* 100' provides a unison entry at bar 87. I have found that ♪ = 90 gives the cor anglais wider scope for the virtuosic display suggested. This makes it possible for the variable tempi of the motivic material to be more clearly conveyed, as hinted earlier. At bar 96 the clarinet is best left without a beat. While the instruction to establish the tempo in bar 100 is loosely suggested as 'at least ♪ = 80', the contrapuntal detail is achieved with exactly that tempo. Once the tempo of ♪ = 112 is established again at bar 110 the events are similar to those already discussed, until bar 157, where all the parts are disparate. Two slow beats can help the co-ordination as long as the rise of the second is slower than the first, to give the required anticipation of the downbeat landing in bar 158. From here to bar 161, one beat to each bar is helpful to the players. At bar 161 it is most effective if the beats required are given in a clear conventional manner. 'As fast as possible' works at ♪ = 120. Beating four in bar 166 helps the players to organise their independent irrational motifs. My solution to bars 167–9 is to combine them as one bar with four beats; the second for the entries of oboe, flute and clarinet; the third for bar 169 entries; the fourth for the last four notes of the clarinet part. This provides an assured silence for the clarinet solo after the dotted bar line. Bar 170 requires two beats and a plateau gesture for the unison rest.

The section beginning at bar 173 is the most complex for the conductor. Each part must sustain the impression of independence. Therefore, the beat must never induce an accentuated response. Geometric shapes, especially lateral, with mostly wrist action, helps to give clarity for the players. They can then sense the inner irregular pulse at each moment. The basic tempo of ♪ = 112 is set at bar 173. Rosbaud symbols are needed with the two beats. Quaver and dotted quaver symbols are best for bars 173–4. In bar 175 think semiquavers at ♪ = 140, but conduct four beats in the following values: $\frac{7+2}{16}$, the pause accounting for the first note of the second 5/16 bar in the cor anglais part. This also accommodates the arrangement for the clarinet. Two quaver beats in bar 176 complete the section. The crossing paths of motivic material continue up to bar 207, where the issues become less complex. Until then, detailed examination of the choreography is essential in learning and preparing the score.

Bar 177 requires two beats at ♪ = 112. The metronome mark of ♪ = 140 in the flute part relates to the quintuplet quaver value. Placing a ruler in a perpendicular angle across the score, focused on the second quaver beat on the clarinet's semiquaver rest, will answer all questions of displacement. The same procedure will resolve the issue with two quaver beats in bar 182. Bar 183 has subdivisions of 3+2+2+2. This can be simplified with three dotted quaver beats at dotted ♪ = 74+. Two quaver beats in bar 184 and one in bar 185 containing a raised beat and a rapid fall into bar 185b, will provide a guide for the motifs in individual parts. It is also useful to enter this beating programme in the free flute part as a demarcation indicator for the unison silent bar. Two beats are needed for bar 186, but allowing freedom to the bassoon on the second prepares for another magic moment of static beauty.

It is important to keep in mind that, while such a preparation for the mechanics of the performance are being established, we must contextualise its creation in Stockhausen's preoccupation with composing what is a pioneering classic in electro-acoustic music – *Gesang der Jünglinge*. This had a profound effect on his approach to instrumental composition. In his own words, '*Zeitmaße* saw the realization of the internal form of my instrumental music.'[18] In a second, more prolonged sustained chord in a central register, all five instruments produce a sudden, very quiet chord with constantly changing dynamics against the single tone of the clarinet. Here, there is a direct imitation of electronic band-filtering. Over almost 5 seconds duration the colour changes produce an incredibly warm glow of sound in total contrast to the 'vibrating swarms of sound' we have been experiencing up to this point.

A strong preparation beat is required to accommodate the grace-note cluster which introduces bar 191. Two beats only are required, but very slow in relation to ♩ = 32. One beat is needed in each of bars 192–4, but again, very slow in relation to the metronome mark ♪ = 64 at bar 191. Conduct three beats in the same time units in bar 195, and one beat in bar 197. It is advisable to control the slow tempo in bar 198 with four beats in obvious places. A new symbol might be adopted in bar 199 to ensure that the oboe, flute and cor anglais secure a sudden, single event, reaching silence at the same time with a plateau gesture at the base of the beat. It is important to provide a short beat at bar 199b because it is indicated in the parts.

In spite of the freedom involved, as stated earlier, Stockhausen has delineated the vertical cohesion he desires in the score. Bar 200 again combines strict pulse in approximate speeds. Taking the oboe's single note as a translation of the time-signature, a 4/4 semibreve specifies a workable recommendation for beating. In bars 201–6 there is no other way of explaining a beating solution, except for direct illustration in Example 43.

The overlapping of bars and time-signatures cannot be rationalised in conventional terminology. To some extent, Stockhausen is expecting the metric calculations of the players to create the perpendicular relationships he so skilfully arranges in the score. For the conductor, preparation involves detailed exercises to ensure that □ (♩), △ (♪.) and ⊓ (♪) values are consistently relevant to the metronome mark ♪ = 64 until the clarinet's ♪ = 112 just before bar 205, where an appropriate adjustment must be made. In order to achieve constant accuracy in the varying pulses of these measures it is best to practise the beating with consistent tempi until you can have a rhythmically unrelated conversation with yourself while conducting the section. Once achieved, you will have gained the automatic physical control required of any technical procedure. This will also facilitate aural concentration on what is happening in the rehearsal. Once at bar 206, in four regular beats at ♪ = 56, the complexity diminishes. As long as the variations in tempo are controlled in the beating manner discussed on p. 43 the requirements are conventional.

At bar 230 the only instrument to have a change of tempo marked is the bassoon: 'at most ♪ = 80'. The other instruments are instructed that the 'bassoon gives the tempo'. In a conducted performance, as a precaution it is wise to place a tempo indication of ♪ = 80 at the top of the page. The beating patterns from here onwards relate to quaver and dotted-quaver units. In bar 149 after four quaver beats the final demisemiquaver should be signalled with a plateau gesture followed by a preparation beat to accommodate the following grace-note clusters, continuing at the stated minimum tempo of ♪ = 136 with the previous beating patterns.

In bars 272–3 Stockhausen asks for instruments to be raised on a grace note and the following quaver in the cor anglais. This is impractical. I recommend raising the instrument on the grace note and lowering it on the main note. This will achieve the 'strongly marked' request. Bar 278 requires only one beat, but with a preparatory gesture for the grace notes. Bar 279 benefits from a single beat with a subsidiary for the cor anglais grace notes.

A rather elegant coda begins at bar 281. It would emphasise the varying dynamic gestures in bar 284 if conducted in three, with an exaggerated *ritardando*. The sudden variations in tempi for which Stockhausen requires 'nuances in steps, not gradations', are related to changes of characterisation. From bar 293 the flowing legato cascades require a velvet-like *piano* in the flow of gestures.

Emphasising the 'clear distinctions' in the clarinet's line at bar 297 indicates the expressive quality which underlines the whole of the coda. There are many more articulation details here which qualify the strong characterisations required. A 'Leichte Töne' instruction for the bassoon at bar 300 is a further illustration of the gentle character required as gradually more and more *legato* phrases are introduced after bar 308, where 'at most *f*' is indicated. This beautiful counterpoint is interrupted suddenly by brittle, explosive articulations which soon ebb into calmness. These two characteristics are sustained in a contradictory fashion, which seem to be questioning the manner of the closure. The final four bars are

EXAMPLE 43 Karlheinz Stockhausen, *Zeitmaße*

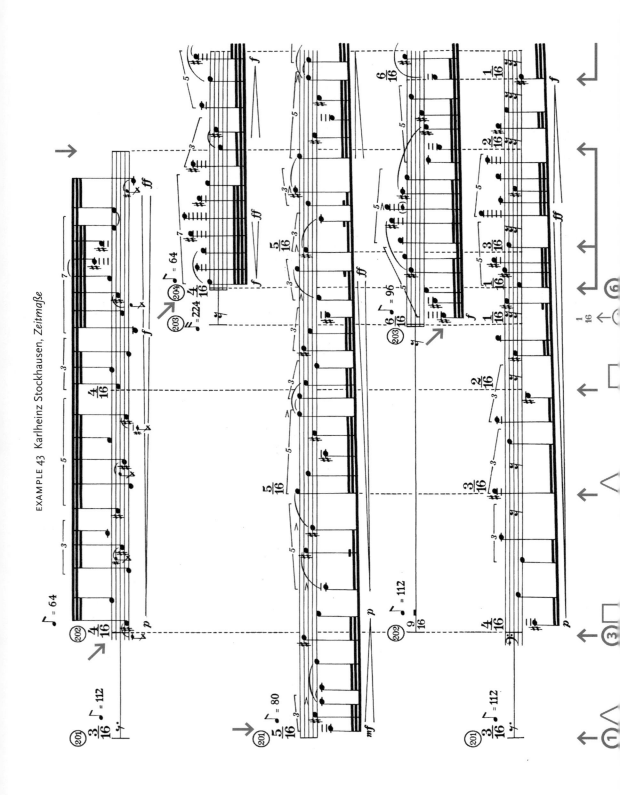

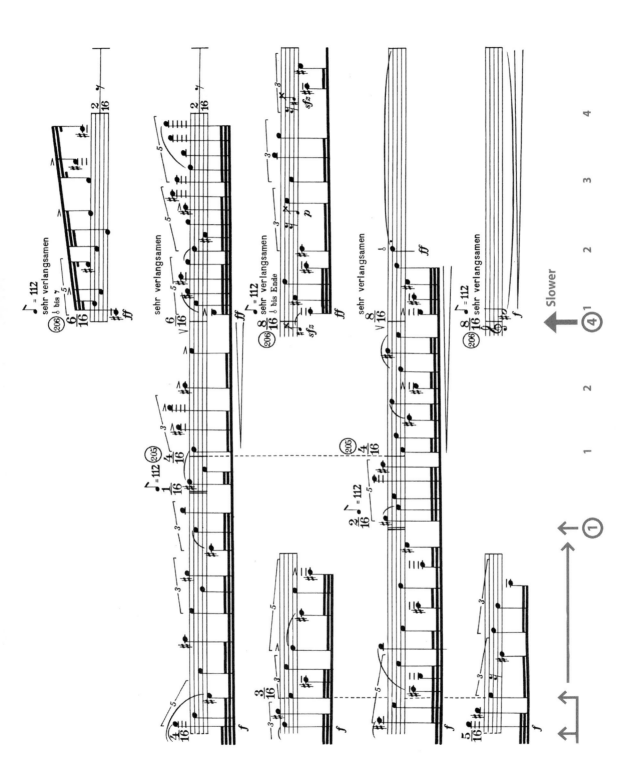

surprisingly simple compared with the complexities explored elsewhere. A strict pulse in rhythmic unison fades into a distant *chalumeau* E from the clarinet.

Two extremes of time relationship govern the work. Closing with a synchronised statement is rather like putting a full stop at the end of a long and convoluted sentence. In the process of determining a mode of conducting which can sustain the sense of five instruments often playing in isolation from each other, the suggestions made should be accompanied by an intimate manner of gesture based on a fairly narrow window of active operation and constantly fluent in the geometry recommended.

Score: Alphonse Leduc, 1966

Of all Messiaen's works, *Couleurs de la cité céleste* is the most challenging to conduct. Once mastered, the techniques involved can be usefully applied to all of the composer's works. It is difficult to think of a piece that is more punctuated by silences. The numerous sections are very much in block formation, each one being quite short but very contrasting in tempo and character, but introduced in quick succession. To gain an overall view of the structure of the work, Robert Sherlaw Johnson's book on Messiaen is invaluable.[19] His Table IX (on p. 180) shows how these block formations relate to each other. Such a vision of the piece is essential to formulating the gestural vocabulary required to conduct it. In spite of the silences punctuating the work, the performance must sustain a fundamental coherence. It is likely that such a design would fail with another composer, but in Messiaen it becomes a successful hallmark.

The symbolism which motivates all Messiaen's works relates to religion in some, nature in some and number in others. But *Couleurs de la cité céleste* contains a synthesis of them all, hence the abrupt and extreme contrast of substance. While Messiaen insists that 'life reveals itself if the work is successful without identification being necessary',[20] I consider it important for a conductor to sensitise the significance of the symbols, in order to characterise the music. Messiaen describes them in conversation with Claude Samuel: 'there is in my music this juxtaposition of Catholic faith, the Tristan and Isolde myth and a highly developed use of bird song'.[21] In *Couleurs de la cité céleste* we can add the rhythmic structures of Indian tâlas, Greek pulses and exotic colours, which feed into the three main symbols. 'Catholic faith' is explained by Messiaen as 'the first aspect of my work, the noblest and, doubtless, the most useful and valuable'.[22] He associates the Tristan and Isolde myth with love in these words: 'I'm sensitive to human love ... the greatest myth of human love [is] Tristan and Isolde.'[23] Birdsong is related to his 'profound love of nature'.[24] In combining these symbols with rhythm and texture Messiaen explains that 'rhythm is music inspired by the movements of nature, movements of free and unequal durations'. It is the primordial nature of rhythm which he considers to have been ignored by composers from 1600 to 1900, with rare exceptions. For him it was *Le Sacre du printemps* which confronted this issue and transformed the evolution of musical language in the twentieth century: 'Rhythm is probably the primordial and perhaps essential part of music: I think it probably existed before melody and harmony'.[25] This is perhaps too broad a generalisation when we consider early precedents already discussed on p. 22. So Stravinsky and Messiaen were not acting upon untried rhythmic concepts, but they were extending their application to much more complex structures. An inducement for Messiaen was the way in which Indian tâlas related to irregularity of pulse. Choosing from a table of 120,[26] we find four of them used within the first five bars of *Couleurs de la cité céleste*: bar 2 'hamasalila', bar 3 'Karanayati', bar 4 'lilâ' and bar 5 'jhaihpâ'. Rhythmic symbols for the conductor are inserted at the outset and must be observed exactly for most of the work. While bars 1 and 9 represent two different birds, it is interesting to note that Messiaen specifies them in the score, but not the tâlas. Religious symbols are represented by the brass choir in four different plainchant melodies. Figure 8 in the score is the first one, in which the Alleluia for the eighth Sunday after Pentecost is signalled *fortissimo* by the piccolo trumpet and cencerros. Below this the seven contrapuntal parts represent the image from the Apocalypse of the seven angels with their seven trumpets. This is the first example which demonstrates the care which a conductor must take in balancing dynamics. The piccolo trumpet and cencerros are set in relief against the ensemble at first, only to be overpowered by the entrance of the bass trombone in the final bar of the statement. Messiaen's footnote even asks for the upper tam-tam to be played *piano* so that it does not affect the resonance of the large tam-tam following at *fortissimo*. These very specific variants become more and more important as the '*couleurs*' enter the textures. The same example shows a variety of note values in each line, most of them derived from individual tâlas. The exceptions lie in the motifs of trumpets 1 and 2, which perform a rhythmic canon on a three-note Cretic rhythm before trumpet 1 diverges from all the other instruments into the irrational rhythms of the tritiya and gajalila tâlas.

The title signifies the overriding element of the work, which is colour association. This is one aspect of a condition known as synaesthesia, in which all the senses are interrelated rather than separate in their functions. A number can have directional associations; a taste can have tactile associations and a sound can have colour associations. These manifestations are purely subjective and vary from one synaesthete to another – a fact which Messiaen failed to appreciate. In naming the colours relating to his vision of the City of God he tells us that he 'noted the names of these colours on the score in order to impress this vision on the conductor who will, in his [her] turn, transmit this vision to the players he [she] directs: the brass should, dare I say it, "play red", the woodwind should "play blue", etc.'[27] Another synaesthete would not necessarily agree with the sound/colour association. This does not minimise the remarkable textures which arise from the orchestration of the 'colour chords' at figure 11 in the score.

In the prefix Messiaen states five quotations from the Apocalypse, three of which refer to colour, especially the fifth, which lists many precious stones. Jasper is particularly significant as representing the 'Holy City'. All the colours of the rainbow and many more are represented in the stones. Figure 11 is magical in effect if all four distinctive dynamics are carefully balanced in rehearsal. Messiaen's instruction for the players gives them a concept of the individual textures required from each group of instruments. If a synaesthete is among them he/she might protest that the sound made is not 'red' or 'blue'. It is the layered dynamics which create the spell: the trumpets extremely quiet; the clarinets slightly more exposed, but in the same register in semitones against the distant trumpets. This is followed by another *pianissimo* chord in the horns and trombone 1, punctuated by a quick-dying *forte* chord high up in the piano register with equally high cencerro *piano* and a high gong colouring the resonances at *mezzo-forte*. Each colour chord statement is burnished with a similar incredible beauty, if balanced explicitly as the composer instructs.

The apogee of textural colour arrives at figure 69, where two of the plainchant Alleluias combine. Messiaen has in mind the effect of brilliant sunlight passing through stained-glass windows. A footnote in the score asks the ensemble to give the impression of abundant colours of stained glass in sunlight. It seems to inform the structure of the work as well. Contrasting sections and textures are shifted suddenly to illuminate each new manifestation of the composer's 'vision', but they are all organically related to it. The *Alleluia de la Dédicase* is played in medieval *organum* by horns and piccolo trumpet with clarinets and cencerros adding chromatic additions to the chords, all played *forte*. In contrast the Alleluia for the 8th Sunday after Pentecost is played *fortissimo* by the piano in chromatic chords. A third element is added *pianissimo* in trumpets, trombones and gongs. The three xylophone instruments punctuate the semiquaver motifs very high at a *piano* level with accents reflecting the piano's Alleluia. These four elements combined, create one of the richest textural creations in the history of music – compelling and beautiful.

Although it seems that the conductor has an easy time at figure 81, keeping an absolutely metronomic beat is just as important here as in the other complex sections. The piano and clarinets have virtuosic individual lines to pursue while the tubular bells play the *Pentecost Alleluia* in quaver quintuplets against the 4/8 signature. Syncopated tâla rhythms cut across this in the cencerros. It is a very exciting episode which opens the way for a coda which recapitulates the main elements of the piece, concluding with a chorale-like statement of the *Saint-Sacrement Alleluia*.

In the second edition of *Le Marteau sans maître* (1957), Boulez was the first composer to illustrate a score with the Rosbaud symbols integrated into the graphics. Their absence in the first edition indicates that the work might not have been conceived with a specific choreography in mind. Boulez includes them in the second edition only as recommendations, not as explicit instructions. This is a wise direction in view of the flexibility of pulse in so many of the movements where gestural language requires many subjective decisions. In *Couleurs de la cité céleste*, Messiaen's concept is closely aligned to the conductor's role, so that the pulse symbols become an imperative aspect of the graphics. There are very few moments where an alternative to the directions in the score might be merited. The technique required is complex. As with *Le Marteau sans maître* directional consistency is imperative.

With a metronome mark of ♪ = 126, initially it is something of a shock to discover that the conductor is required to beat in semiquavers (♪ = 252!). The time-signature in bar 1 is a conventional 3/16. From bar 2 time-signatures identify individual units written within the bar, even when irregular. This nomenclature is essential to an understanding of the intensity of pulse relationships in Messiaen's music. The second bar might well have been written as 6/32, but this would not feel the same in preparing for the unequal units of bars 3–5. While recognising the break with convention in the notation and conducting symbols, the principle is consistent with the notational decisions made by much earlier composers. For instance, if a pianist plays the second E♭ Impromptu of Schubert so fast that the figurations no longer sound like triplets, the pulse innate to the harmonic structure is lost. It is exactly the same in Messiaen's work, in which rapid phrases with irregular pulse units require exactly the same rhythmic impulse. The conductor *must* sensitise this facet and relate it to physical gesture if the complexity of the rhythmic structure is to be effective. The fundamental ingredient for achieving rhythmic accuracy is discussed in relation to *Le Sacre du printemps* (p. 23) but in Messiaen we have to relate it to the intensely rapid tempi. While the height of the 'triangle' beat has to be greater than the 'open box', the shape of the beat must be geometric rather than arched. The players require very clear shapes in the geometry, especially in the consistency of the central focus for the downbeat and related gestures. This is particularly important in bars 3 and 4 where the upbeat is very rapid. If it is too low the downbeat will be late at such a fast tempo. The geometry requires that the upbeat should always be higher than the others as if gently striking a perpendicular line as opposed to the horizontal base of all other beats.

As with instrumental practice it is often necessary to separate technical characteristics from the artistic in order to gain muscular autonomy before applying a technical facet to the music. A useful exercise is as follows:

1 Establish a floating arm position free from tension with a central focus for the downbeat.

2 While sustaining a two-unit shape, practise ⌐△ with the varying height and speed of each unit, remembering to keep the upbeat on the second one higher than the base beat. Using differing vocal syllables to distinguish the downbeat from subsidiary beats (e.g. da-ga/da-ga-der) articulate them together with the physical action to develop a strong sense of the rapid subdivisions of each unit. This is related to the way in which an Indian tabla player illustrates the complexities of tâla rhythms. It is directly related to Messiaen's rhythmic patterns in this and other works of his.

3 Reverse the process described in 2 (△⌐). Because of the extremely rapid upbeat in this formation it is easy for the downbeat to land late. Therefore it is imperative to strike the rapid upbeat very high on the perpendicular line described earlier. If the beat is too low, the upward swing will be too large to accommodate the downbeat in time.

4 Practise conducting alternating units of ⌐△ | △⌐ in quick succession, vocalising the varying subdivisions at first, then just thinking them, then just thinking of the main alternating units without subdivisions. In other words, simply rely on the practised physical patterns to determine the precise duration of each unit.

5 Once a sense of physical control of the two beating patterns has
been achieved at an automatic level, improvise an unrhythmic
verbal conversation independent of the beating patterns. This
will help independence of physical gesture from the listening
process. Ultimately this becomes an invaluable tool which
creates the facility for listening to what is happening in
rehearsal, as stated elsewhere.

Olivier Messiaen,
Couleurs de la
cité céleste

A conductor must *never* have to consider or think of a gesture in rehearsal
or a performance. Choreography is part of the learning process in
digesting a score, just as fingering is part of the learning process for an
instrumentalist. Gestural decisions are an essential part of the learning
process, especially in the music under discussion. Autonomy of gesture
is an imperative technical requirement in all music of this kind.

Pursuing the principle of a preparatory gesture, not a beat, as
discussed on p. 19, the pulse of ♪ = 252 cannot be used for this purpose
because it is too fast for players to respond to effectively. At the opening,
and in similar sections throughout the work, the preparatory lift must be
a quaver, which is, as Messiaen indicates, the foundation pulse for this
material.

It is puzzling that in many performances and recordings of the
work, it is not the most challenging aspects which suffer problems, but
the deceptively simple moments, such as figure 11. At the slow pulse
of ♪ = 50 the unison articulations often fail to be unison. The conductor
has a number of issues to consider in resolving the problem. While
the varying dynamics and registers of the instrumental groups are
important features in achieving the textures implied, gestures have to
be formulated which take into account differing forms of articulation
in each instrumental group. In the first chord the clarinets will give a
cushioned *piano* articulation ('bwaa' might describe it) while the trumpets
and trombones will be slightly more incisive. In the second chord the
horns are high and will be rather like the clarinets when articulating at
a *pianissimo* level. They are punctuated by a sharp *forte* chord from the
piano and cencerros, which are percussively incisive, while the gong will
be less immediate with the slight swell of its 'bwaa'-type attack, generated
by the resonating harmonics of the metal. A slow beat at ♪ = 50, even
if obeying the bouncing ball principle, will not produce the unison

chord, containing so many different articulations and dynamics, which makes this moment so beautiful. The following points offer a solution. The swing of the percussion strokes should identify with the intake of breath by the wind players. It is helpful if a conductor is sensitive to this form of preparation for an articulation, reflecting it in the preparatory gesture. With four slow quavers to the bar, the first should be initiated with a preparatory subdivided quaver lift which will fall fast and remain static at the base before a similar semiquaver preparation for the second chord, giving the feeling, but not the action of a subdivided quaver. The intake of breath and preparation of the percussion swing, together with the immediacy of the piano chord, requires conscious empathy in the manner of the conductor's gesture. I have found that asking the pianist and cencerros player to be a little 'lazy' in the attack helps them to be aware of the varying articulations which they punctuate. Sustaining the rich warmth of the chords in the third and fourth units of each bar can be achieved by ghosting the beats with the right hand while suspending the left hand high. The 'colour chords' are magic only when articulated precisely by all instruments. Messiaen's role as an organist might have something to do with the mixtures he creates in such beautiful chordal motifs. In ensemble, it is the conductor who must understand and generate the beauty of such mixture, which informs the whole work. This is especially important in the Alleluias, in which quality of tone in the brass is more important than volume. It is tempting for these players to blaze away in such glorious moments, whether *f* or *ff*. A beautiful tone, with dignity and *cantabile* resonance, is essential. But above all, the articulation should be with sustained legato tonguing, avoiding accentuation. The *tenuto* signs are indicative of such a characterisation.

The issue of continuity in this very sectionalised piece is especially important at such places as in figure 13, where the previous section runs straight into the new, slower tempo without any preparation. This relates to the principle that a sudden change of pulse is controlled by the manner in which the conductor moves from the first beat of a new, unprepared tempo to the second. In this case the final beat of the section preceding figure 13 is considerably faster than the new slow tempo. The pulse for the new tempo is established after the downbeat while moving with a much higher arch to the second beat. While ♪ = 80 is a very small unit for the new pulse, it is essential to beat with this throughout the section. The reverse of this procedure follows soon at figure 14. In the bar before this, while the tempo is very slow, there is time to remain still at the base of the second beat, so that a rapid preparation for figure 14 can be made for the ♪ = 252 beats required. There must be no break between these two sections if the mosaic is not to fall apart. The exception to this procedure is in the bar before figure 17. As this is a silent bar it can be treated as a GP, involving a preparation at the pulse of the new section, ♪ = 126. It is a useful calculation to judge the tempo of the first dotted semiquaver beat at figure 21 and to compare it with the ♪ = 120 pulse of the previous bar. At ♪ = 126 the dotted semiquaver value of the first △ beat at figure 21 is ♪. = 168, followed by the semiquaver at 252. This 'change of gear' must be learned exactly in order to sustain the consistency of pulse in each repeated motif. Again, the very fast rise of the first beat must anticipate the exact displacement of the second. The varying heights of △ and ⊓ as practised earlier will be invaluable at the time when this becomes intuitive and not calculated.

The section beginning at figure 27 contains seven different metronome marks within twelve bars, each of which is extreme in contrast, although linked. These tempi must be exact if the integration of the motifs is to achieve coherence within the statement. Articulation details are equally important. The semiquavers in the brass statement at figure 29 are deceptive. They are slower than they appear and should be fully sustained notes with linear character, not separated. Messiaen has written the first bar of figure 30 as a ratio of 9:8 in the clarinets and piano parts, but notated it as groups of 4, 2 and 3 demisemiquavers against regular sextuplet figures in the marimba part. Strictly speaking, the fifth note of the 9:8 group should be articulated fractionally before the second group of sextuplets. The beaming seems to complicate the issue. If the last beat of the previous section is halted at the base of the beat, a swift preparation for the new tempo will give the players a cue to play as fast as possible. The resulting 9 against 12 will not be an issue at such a speed. As a final observation on this matter, the second horn will be able to control the long *diminuendo* over two bars before figure 31 more comfortably if the attack is *f* rather than *ff*. The trombone will compensate for this with its comparatively shorter note in a more comfortable register.

199

Olivier Messiaen,

Couleurs de la

cité céleste

In the section at figure 38 Messiaen instructs the conductor to beat semiquavers in the 3/16 and 2/16 bars, which means ♪ = 288! I find this to be impractical. Players find it much more helpful to have these bars beaten in 1. The same applies to the bar before figure 39.

With semiquaver beats at figure 41 the 4/16 bar before figure 42 needs only one pause beat, so that a steady preparation can be made for this central section of the work. Paradoxically, the straightforward four in a bar for the whole section is intensely demanding because the various groups of players have exact entries at differing points in all four subdivisions of the quaver unit. The hemidemisemiquavers in the xylophone part will collapse if the conductor is one hemidemisemiquaver out of synchronisation. Accomplishing such mechanical accuracy can only be achieved by listening and mentally playing the parts with the instruments. If the concept is not exact this will intrude on all the other instrumental groups. It is wise not to underestimate the skill required to achieve this exactitude.

At figure 55 conducting two beats at the rapid tempo is advisable. Messiaen recommends leaving the piano to its own devices for two bars. A preparation on the second beat of the pianist's second bar secures the attack at figure 57, a repetition of the 'abyss' motif.

Following the *Pentecost Alleluia* at figure 72, the colour chords are marked '*extatique*'. This qualification can only be achieved if the dynamic balancing of the chords is carefully sensitised, with brass as quiet as possible and clarinets providing 'floating' articulations. It is important not to make the pauses any longer than instructed. The graphic durations are deceptively long. The preparation should mime the intake of the players' breath, which is always taken in and held slightly before the articulation. The piano/percussion in the second bar requires a subdivision of the first beat. In the third bar it is more effective to place the second beat on the dotted semiquaver pause, releasing the sustained chord in exact displacement of the articulated chord.

At figure 81 all the symbols are represented in this vivid contrapuntal display. Each of the instruments has an individual role in their motivic characterisations, which defy any sense of regular pulse in spite of the consistent four-unit bars. As at figure 42 the conductor has to be an intensely strict metronome if the counterpoint is to make sense. It is a wonderful *dénouement* for the whole work in its virtuosity and rhythmic diversity – a truly inspired climax. What follows is a compressed recapitulation of all the previous material, culminating in a glorious and resonant *Alleluia du Saint-Sacrement*. This must retain a warm dignity of tone from the brass, nothing blatant or forced, simply elegant and beautiful. The conductor's demeanour should evoke this quality in order to bring a noble coda to this work.

☐ ☐ ☐ ☐

Harrison Birtwistle, Silbury Air

Scores: Universal Edition, 1979; revised version 2003

Issues of pulse have inevitably been prominent in a book relating to music of the twentieth and twenty-first centuries. It has also been stressed that subjective artistry should never be absent from any technical mechanism required for interpretation and performance. Nonetheless, there is a further dimension to analyse in relation to pulse itself. In Part One the music of several composers illustrates varying applications of metric modulation. An extreme experiment with this feature is made by Harrison Birtwistle in what could be described as a pulse piece. His *Silbury Air* makes very exacting, but very exciting demands on a conductor. There are two versions of the work: the original dating from 1979 and a revised one from 2003. Both editions are required for reference; I shall refer to the 1979 version as A, the 2003 as B. In A there is a unique graphic characteristic which identifies the number of beats in any bar by a single integer, while the quality of the units is signified by a time-signature. B simplifies the complex irregularity of pulse by using conventional notation. Comparing pp. 1 and 2 in each version exposes a number of varying features. Throughout B Birtwistle has chosen to revise some of the orchestration and to recompose certain sections. While the revised version B must now be used in performance, I consider it to be essential for a conductor to study version A because its structural relation to the pulse labyrinth, printed as a glossary in both versions, is more identifiable with the composition process than version B.

From a composer's point of view, version A contains a fascinating logic which a conductor will also find useful in gaining an insight into the motivation behind Birtwistle's idea. He describes the substance as 'invested logic via modes of juxtaposition, modes of repetition, modes of change'. The pulse labyrinth sets out the metric modulation relationships. In version B Birtwistle explains that this is included to indicate the 'compositional logic' rather than an aid for conductors. I maintain that the labyrinth is an essential part of the conductor's comprehension of the music. It is also useful as a practice aid for the metric relationships to be controlled in the piece.

Initially, the score-learning process involves constant mental subdivision of each unit prescribed. In version A the opening metronome mark of ♩ = 90 must be mentally subdivided by four semiquavers, preparing for the slower pulse of ♩♪ = 72 at bar 15, where the unit is subdivided into five, with ♪ = ♪, then back to ♩ = 90 at bar 17, completing the cycle with ♩. = 120 in bar 18. This relates to the second set of metric relationships in labyrinth IV. In this version the integers specifying the number of beats in each measure require the same varying directional downbeats discussed on p. 153, also to the automatic control of the varying height of each subdivision, which is an imperative technical requirement in such a work. At figure 1 in the A score a dotted quaver becomes equal to a crotchet in a 4/16 unit, thus reverting to the second set of semiquaver subdivisions.

In version B, time-signatures take on their conventional role with occasional qualifications of the varying units in added integers, as in bars 15 and 18, creating a need for the rather less conventional time-signature of 15/16, although with a varying number of beats to a bar. The result establishes exactly the same conducting requirements as in version A.

As an aspect of the structural mechanism of the piece it can be helpful at places where the labyrinth relationships change (such as bars 20 and 28) to use a code marking to indicate that the tempo of the pulse does not change, only the subdivision. My own code is 'LS' (*lo stesso tempo*). It is also interesting to note that figure 3 has a metronome mark of 144, which only appears in its diminished relationship of 72 in the labyrinth. The logic of this results in the latter appearing at figure 4. 'LS' appears in my score and in score B in bars 46 and 49. This might be the only time a composer has ever used 25/16 as a time-signature.

The individual routes taken by the double basses at 4 and the cellos at 5 should be freely articulated at the tempo established in rehearsal. This sets the conducted tempo taken by the *subito ffff* brass at bar 54, in a Lutosławski-like polyphony. A left-hand cue for the cellos and double basses at 6 will provide the demarcation required for them to re-enter the conducted ensemble.

From figure 8 'LS' signals are useful to have in the score at bars 89, 92, 97 and at several subsequent metric junctions where metronome mark 90 is indicated as a norm up to bar 113. At figure 9 when the basic unit becomes a dotted quaver, version A supplies the metronome mark of 67.5 for the crotchet unit in the second bar, as specified in the labyrinth. While time-signatures revert to their conventional function in the B version Birtwistle does not completely abandon the use of integers to clarify many of the pulse relationships. The sections from figures 12–16 and 25–8 in version B show considerable changes from A in barring and displacement of notes within the bars. The problem which had to be resolved in conducting the A version was the number of single-beat bars of varying subdivisions from one bar to another. No matter how accurate the conductor's directing it was extremely difficult for the players to sustain an accurate response to constantly varying beats which were all downbeats. My own solution in directing the work in this original form was to conduct the 3/16 and 2/16 bars as 5/16 bars with two beats in order to create identifiable contrasts of beat direction. In version B this dilemma provides similar solutions but with displacement changes in the rhythmic punctuation.

At figure 12 the B version simplifies the process of beating but, as in version A, the constant variations from bar to bar of two, three, four and five divisions of single beat units is extremely difficult for the players to follow. The new barring in B requiring only one quintuplet unit in the section (bar 126) is a good solution. With a metronome mark of ♩ ♪ = 72, bar 126 is very much slower than the 9/16 bar at ♪. = 120. Therefore it is appropriate to subdivide the former into beats of ♪. = 150 and ♪ = 180. At figure 14, when the crotchet becomes 72, I still recommend similar subdivisions of the units in 5/16 bars with ♪ = 144 and ♪. = 96. This also assists the brass while counting bars rest for their entry at figure 15 (assisted by a left-hand cue). When the dotted quaver modulates to ♩ ♪ = 96 at bar 47 there is no other solution but to beat one in a bar consistently, but with immaculate variety of height in each beat to distinguish the differing values until bar 58, when subdivisions in all but 3/16 bars are helpful to the players. As the pace slows it is important to subdivide in 5/16 and 4/16 bars which are respectively ♩ = 54 and ♩ ♪ = 43.2, so that two bars before figure 16, the value of the bar is twice that of figure 16 itself. At this point there is a span of ten beats within one bar in version A. Version B rationalises it into three separate bars up to bar 178, which requires a calculation of the dotted crotchet beat at 72.

From the beginning up to figure 16, version B establishes practical revisions which aid the conductor and the players. From this point some of the barring has been redesigned, especially after figure 17, when version B at bar 198 contains a metronome mark which calls for an 'LS' sign to sustain exactly the same pulse. Strong rhythmic exactitude in the beating keeps the jagged motifs in the brass incisive and exciting – especially in the rhythmic polyphony after figure 20, where both versions of the score are the same up to one bar before figure 22. With the tempo at ♩ = 72 it is important to recognise that the 5/16 bars beginning at figure 22 are at a very slow ♩ ♪ = 57.6, requiring a very high arch in the beat for the explosive effect of the entries. At the eighth bar of figure 23, version A is designated as 4/8 + 2/3. This is the result of crossed displacements of triplet quavers. Version B (bar 264) rationalises this into a 4/12 bar. This process is repeated in the A version two bars later in 5/8 + 2/3 and 5/12 in version B. In both cases the units are extended making the quaver displacements a little longer. Version B offers the solution with four and five beats respectively.

The section from figures 25–8 has been touched on briefly. The B version combines 5/16 and 2/16 bars into 7/16. The 4/16 bar becomes a 2/8 to alleviate the problem of so many rapid and varied single beat bars. My own preference is to use rapid ⊓ and △ beats at ♪ = 225 (the crotchet being 112.5 in relation to the specified ♩ ♪ = 90). This is still slower than the 252 speed in Messiaen's *Couleurs de la cité céleste* and creates a recognisable subdivision of individual bars for the players. When the metronome mark at bar 288 makes 5/16 into 112.5 there is no alternative in either version but to give a single beat to each bar until bar 297 (5/16×12 in the A version). From figure 26 the B version creates practical solutions in the barring with the proviso that 5/16 and 3/16 bars should be beaten in one. Figures 27–8 require the same process.

The challenges for a conductor examining the initial process of composition in version A are by no means resolved in the later version, in which sacrifices had to be made for practical purposes. Conventional time-signatures change the graphic impression of the score and cannot replace the impact of irregular pulse relationships which Birtwistle's elegant manuscript provided in the first score. These original challenges *can* be met by conductors who empathise with the adventurous spirit which informs the music. Such conductors would be well placed in providing appropriate teaching methods in music colleges. This work is also ideal for formulating the physical control and subtle nuances of gesture in projecting the artistic concept of, not only pulse, but also the textural and poetic content of such a work. The title refers to a prehistoric mound in Wiltshire, England. Birtwistle denies any 'romantic reflection' in the title, aligning the motivation for the piece more with Paul Klee's *Imaginary Landscape*. Such imagery is the starting point for a conductor in learning the work.

Returning to the mechanism, figure 32 presents an aleatory feature which interrupts the punctuated rhythmic schemes which inform the music up to this point. With the exception of the double bass part the strings are dissociated from the conductor's control most of the time. A crotchet qualification for the speed is added in version B, which also modifies the conductor's beat for the rest of the ensemble. In either version the aim for the strings that pursue aleatory motifs is to create a complex polyphony from individual choices which the instructions indicate. The entry of the special 'drum' is secured by a swift preparation for the downbeat at the second bar. This also applies to the entry one beat before figure 33. My recommendation in cueing the *subito ffff* and *pppp* for the aleatory strings, while conducting with regular beats for the rest of the ensemble, is to divide responsibility between the hands. Time beating relating to time-signatures should be done only with the right hand. The left should cue such drum entries with a plateau gesture. Aleatory strings should be instructed to follow left-hand cues only, so that the *subito* entries can be uniform. The explosive interruptions to the peaceful backdrop of the *pppp* sections require incisive rhythmic assertion, especially between figures 34 and 37, where the barring has been reorganised in version B, so that crotchet units become the main pulse element. Again, the beating should be allocated to the right hand. In deciding whether or not to subdivide the shorter unit bars it is important to establish that the main unit is ♩ = 160, whereas the dotted quaver = 213.3. My own preference is to beat both of these as single beats using the manner of beating for *Couleurs de la cité céleste* (p. 195). The exception to this is the 5/16 bar, which requires only one beat. A useful way of practising the varying height of beats in crotchet + semiquaver, crotchet and dotted quaver units in this section is to establish the crotchet unit at 160 while articulating semiquaver subdivisions with d-g-d-g consonants. With the 5/16 bars, thinking of ⊓ △ graphics, the articulations will be d-g/d-g-d, and simply d-g-d for the dotted quaver. Increasing and decreasing the height of the varying units will soon become automatic and the articulations can be dispensed with.

At figure 33 the percussionist has five bars in a dominant role as loud as possible. In version A the player is then instructed to slowly raise the right hand followed by left hand in the same action. It is a dramatic preparation for the explosive attack in the bar before figure 34. This instruction is absent in version B, the single drum stroke being replaced by a *crescendo* of grace notes into the powerful articulation. These grace notes in the B version render the arm-raising action inappropriate because of the crescendo from *mf*. As a dramatic gesture the arm-raising was impressive. But the replacement by the grace-note sextuplet is equally exciting. In the pause bar before figure 34 the percussion attack should be indicated with the simple raising of the arm in preparation for an upbeat gesture, giving the percussionist an exact anticipation of where this will land in focusing the grace notes. At figure 35 it is important to remind oneself that the dotted quaver unit is 213.3, following the ♩ = 160 preparation related to the drum stroke and at all such events up to figure 37. I recommend using only the right hand in beating for instruments with time-signatures. Instructing the players performing the aleatory elements to respond to left indications for the *subito* dynamic changes, will achieve the desired effect. It is recommended that left-hand signs be placed in the score to secure consistency in this signalling. The demarcation point at figure 38 should be preceded in the previous bar by three beats (indicated in the score and parts) with the left hand, to establish the new ♩ = 40 tempo for everyone. The added half unit in this bar is simply to indicate consistency with the metric modulation principle.

The unwinding of the aleatory parts in the gradual slowing of the metric metres is an aspect dependent to some extent on the pulse indications for the strings and harp, provided by the first violinist, while the conductor sustains the beat for the instrumentalists with time-signatures. In version A the conductor is provided with specific pulse instructions following the percussion entry in this section. Version B dispenses with it. By sustaining the conductor's role for parts with time-signatures in the right hand a dichotomy of tempi between the parts develops as groups depart from the initial tempo. The conductor will reduce the speed to ♩ = 120 at the brass entry in bar 449, while signalling points of tempo change in the aleatory parts with the left hand. In bar 448 it is important to marry with the percussion part for beats three and four. Ghosting the beat in this bar will give the percussionist freedom to lead into the new alignment with the conductor's beat.

In rehearsing the aleatory sections many questions are likely to be asked by the players. It saves rehearsal time if the conductor divides the ensemble for sections which have equivalent tempo changes. This is especially helpful to the very long improvisational aspects for the strings. When a change of speed is indicated this will be established by the conductor, while he/she is also indicating the left-hand signals for *subito* dynamic changes. This also gives the players practice in choosing the varying order of their segments. It would also be helpful to pursue this method in more than one rehearsal. Once the varying tempi have been established the first violinist can take over the role for indicating each new pulse in relation to the conductor's left-hand signals.

The individual layers of motivic substance and texture are woven with great skill and imagination by the composer. In realising the work, the conductor's exactitude in controlling the pulse elements must go beyond the role of time-beating. That is why the technical requirements must become automatic in the process of learning the score. The characterisation of the events in the subjective language of the conductor's technique is equally as important in this work as in one by Tchaikovsky. Players can be very adept at responding well to direction in a work of this kind if the conductor's technique is consistent, absent from tension and clear in the geometry of beating. These are the basic requirements. Beyond this is the fleshing of the skeleton of technique. The complex mechanism of this work is an essential ingredient of its expression. In the whispering articulations of the coda the gradual *diminuendo* to *pppp* is accompanied by an equally gradual increase in the pulse articulations, so that the gentle 'blush' of the final *crescendo* towards the harp's bell-like chords is the most unlikely, but remarkable and inventive close to the work.

▢ ▢ ▢ ▢

In Part Three I have concentrated on ensemble rather than orchestral works. The reason for this is that the kind of works analysed are more extreme in their technical demands than those in the orchestral repertoire. Even the orchestral works of Boulez are less complex than his ensemble compositions. The revisions which he made in the scoring of *Pli selon pli* are indicative of the general perception of composers in recognising the time restraints of rehearsal schedules for orchestral works. Complexity in itself is not a virtue, but it can be the route to a good idea. Consequently, there is no reason why the issues of complex ensemble works should not be transferred to the full orchestra. If a conductor is skilful enough to unwrap the complexities for the cultured musicians who inhabit our symphony orchestras the prospects are unlimited.

The works chosen for discussion in Part One are by composers who have stepped outside the conventional world in seeking a vocabulary which expresses new and exploratory directions in their work. Just as composers such as Beethoven, Wagner and Debussy explored new sound worlds and unexplored structural designs, they have presented the conductor with the challenge to comprehend the aspirations of their creative endeavours. They need conductors who can meet such a challenge.

The second half of the twentieth century saw electronics enter the creative world of composers. In the twenty-first century the developing interactive relationship between instruments, voices and electronics is a constantly evolving language. The conductor is part of that evolutionary process and should embrace it.

The recommendations I have made aim at expanding the technical resources required for conducting many kinds of music composed after 1950. However, their application is also intended to enhance the expressive and stylistic performance of music of *all* periods. But an enquiring concern for the music of a conductor's own time is of paramount importance in a constantly changing world.

□ □ □ □

INTRODUCTION

1 Carl Bamberger, *The Conductor's Art* (New York: McGraw-Hill Book Co., 1965), p. 268.

2 Cécile Gilly, *Boulez on Conducting: Conversations with Cécile Gilly*, trans. Richard Stokes (London: Faber & Faber, 2003), p. 129.

3 Bamburger, *The Conductor's Art*, p. 170.

4 Gilly, *Boulez on Conducting*, p. 130.

5 Hermann Scherchen, *Handbook of Conducting*, trans. M. D. Calvacoressi (London: Oxford University Press, 1935), p. 5.

6 Wilhelm Furtwängler, *Notebooks, 1924–1954*, trans. Shaun Whiteside, ed. Michael Tanner (London: Quartet Books, 1989), p. 213.

7 Norman Lebrecht, *The Maestro Myth: Great Conductors in Pursuit of Power* (London: Simon & Schuster, 1992), p. 25.

PART ONE

1 George Grove, motto for the Royal College of Music.

2 Scherchen, *Handbook of Conducting*.

3 Adrian Boult, *A Handbook on the Technique of Conducting* (Oxford: Hall the Printer, 1937), p. 9.

4 Gilly, *Boulez on Conducting*, p. 97

5 Pierre Boulez, *Orientations: Collected Writings*, ed. Jean-Jacques Nattiez, trans. Martin Cooper (London: Faber & Faber, 1986), p. 176.

6 John Cage, 'To Describe the Process of Composition Used in *Music for Piano 21–52*', *Die Reihe* 3 (1957; English language edition 1959), p. 41.

7 Pierre Boulez, 'Aléa', *Perspectives of New Music* 3 (1964), pp. 42–53.

8 Ove Nordwall, ed., *Lutosławski*, trans. Christopher Gibbs (Stockholm: Wilhelm Hanson, 1968), p. 69.

9 András Bálint Varga, *Lutosławski Profile: Witold Lutosławski in Conversation with András Bálint Varga* (London: Chester Music, 1976), p. 51.

PART TWO

Notes

1 Gilly, *Boulez on Conducting*, p. 126.

2 Ibid., p. 105.

3 *Beethoven's Letters*, trans. J. S. Shedlock, selected and edited by A. Eaglefield-Hull (New York: Dover Publications, 1972), pp. 233–4.

4 Antony Pay, *Composer* 69 (Spring 1980), p. 15.

5 Richard Wagner, *On Conducting*, trans. Edward Dannreuther, 4th edition (London: William Reeves, 1940), p. 19.

6 Christopher Adey, *Orchestral Performance: A Guide for Conductors and Players* (London: Faber & Faber, 1998).

7 Gilly, Boulez on Conducting, p. 130.

8 Erich Leinsdorf, *On Music* (Portland, OR: Amadeus Press, 1997), p. 43.

PART THREE

1 Célestin Deliège, *Pierre Boulez: Conversations with Célestin Deliège* (London: Eulenberg Books, 1976), p. 55.

2 Ibid., p. 56.

3 Ibid., p. 66.

4 Ibid., p. 64.

5 Ibid., p. 67.

6 Boulez, *Orientations*, p. 330.

7 Ibid., p. 339.

8 Ibid., p. 341.

9 Ibid., p. 341.

10 Ibid., pp. 330–43.

11 Ibid., p. 340.

12 Ibid., p. 341.

13 Ibid., p. 342.

14 Karl H. Wörner, *Stockhausen: Life and Work*, trans. Bill Hopkins (London: Faber & Faber, 1973), p. 229.

15 Karlheinz Stockhausen, '... how time passes ...', *Die Reihe* 3 (1957; English language edition 1959), p. 10.

16 Wörner, *Stockhausen: Life and Work*, pp. 36–7.

17 Ibid., p. 37.

18 Ibid.

19 Robert Sherlaw Johnson, *Messiaen* (London: J. M. Dent & Sons, 1975)

20 Samuel, Claude, *Conversations with Olivier Messiaen*, trans. Felix Aprahamian (London: Stainer & Bell, 1976), p. 63.

21 Ibid., p. 3.

22 Ibid., p. 2.

23 Ibid., p. 2.

24 Ibid., p. 3.

25 Ibid., p. 33.

26 Sherlaw Johnson, *Messiaen*.

27 Samuel, *Conversations with Olivier Messiaen*, p. 96.

Adey, Christopher, *Orchestral Performance: A Guide for Conductors and Players* (London: Faber & Faber, 1998)

Badal, James, *Recording the Classics: Maestros, Music, Technology* (Kent, OH: Kent State University Press: 1996)

Bamberger, Carl, *The Conductor's Art* (New York: McGraw-Hill Book Co., 1965)

Bartolozzi, Bruno, *New Sounds for Woodwind*, 2nd edn (London: Oxford University Press, 1982)

Beament, James, *The Violin Explained: Components, Mechanism and Sound* (Oxford: Oxford University Press, 1997)

Beethoven, Ludwig van, *Beethoven's Letters*, trans. J. S. Shedlock, selected and edited by A. Eaglefield-Hull (New York: Dover Publications, 1972)

Beyer, Anders, ed., *The Music of Per Nørgård: Fourteen Interpretative Essays* (Aldershot: Scolar Press, 1996)

Blades, James, *Percussion Instruments and their History* (London: Faber & Faber, 1970)

Boretz, Benjamin, and Edward T. Cone, eds., *Perspectives on Notation and Performance* (New York: W. W. Norton & Co., 1976)

Boulez, Pierre, *Orientations: Collected Writings*, ed. Jean-Jacques Nattiez, trans. Martin Cooper (London: Faber & Faber, 1986)

Boult, Adrian, *A Handbook on the Technique of Conducting* (Oxford: Hall the Printer, 1937)

Burgess, Geoffrey, and Bruce Haynes, *The Oboe* (New Haven, CT: Yale University Press, 2004)

Collins, Nick, and Julio d'Escriván, eds., *The Cambridge Companion to Electronic Music* (Cambridge: Cambridge University Press, 2007)

Cottrell, Stephen, *The Saxophone* (New Haven, CT: Yale University Press, 2012)

Cummings, Barton, *The Contemporary Tuba* (New London, CT: Whaling Music Publishers, 1984)

Dean, Roger T., ed., *The Oxford Handbook of Computer Music* (Oxford: Oxford University Press, 2009)

Deliège, Célestin, *Pierre Boulez: Conversations with Célestin Deliège* (London: Eulenberg Books, 1976)

Dempster, Stuart, *The Modern Trombone* (Berkeley: University of California Press, 1979)

Dingle, Christopher, *Messiaen's Final Works* (Farnham: Ashgate Publishing, 2013)

Furtwängler, Wilhelm, *Notebooks, 1924–1954*, trans. Shaun Whiteside, ed. Michael Tanner (London: Quartet Books, 1989)

Gilly, Cécile, *Boulez on Conducting: Conversations with Cécile Gilly*, trans. Richard Stokes (London: Faber & Faber, 2003)

Girsberger, Russ, *A Practical Guide to Percussion Terminology* (Fort Lauderdale, FL: Meredith Music Publications, 1998)

Goossens, Léon, and Edwin Roxburgh, *Oboe*, Yehudi Menuhin Music Guides (London: Kahn & Averill, 1999)

Griffiths, Paul, *Peter Maxwell Davies* (London: Robson Books, 1982)

Grosbayne, Benjamin, *Techniques of Modern Orchestral Conducting* (Cambridge, MA, Harvard University Press, 1973)

Hall, Michael, *Harrison Birtwistle* (London: Robson Books, 1984)

—— *Harrison Birtwistle in Recent Years* (London: Robson Books, 1998)

Hart, Philip, *Conductors: A New Generation* (London: Robson Books, 1980)

Herbert, Trevor, *The Trombone* (New Haven, CT: Yale University Press, 2006)

Holland, James, *Percussion*, Yehudi Menuhin Music Guides (MacDonald and Jane, London, 1978)

Johnson, Robert Sherlaw, *Messiaen* (London: J. M. Dent & Sons, 1975)

Lawson, Colin, ed., *The Cambridge Companion to the Clarinet* (Cambridge: Cambridge University Press, 1995) [including discussions of contemporary clarinet and bass clarinet music by Roger Heaton and Michael Harris respectively]

Lebrecht, Norman, *The Maestro Myth: Great Conductors in Pursuit of Power* (London: Simon & Schuster, 1992)

Leinsdorf, Erich, *On Music* (Portland, OR: Amadeus Press, 1997)

—— *The Composer's Advocate: A Radical Orthodoxy for Musicians* (New Haven, CT: Yale University Press, 1981)

Lewis, Thomas P. *Something about the Music: Guide to Contemporary Repertory*, 4 vols (White Plains, NY: Pro/Am Music Resources; London: Khan & Averill, 1990)

Maconie, Robin, *The Works of Karlheinz Stockhausen* (London: Oxford University Press, 1976)

Matossian, Nouritza, *Xenakis* (London: Kahn & Averill, 1990)

May, Thomas, ed., *The John Adams Reader: Essential Writings on an American Composer* (Pompton Plains, NJ: Amadeus Press, 2006)

Mertens, Wim, *American Minimal Music*, trans. J. Hautekiet (London: Khan & Averill, 1983)

Nelson, Sheila, *The Violin and Viola* (New York: W. W. Norton & Co., 1972)

Nordwall, Ove, ed., *Lutosławski*, trans. Christopher Gibbs (Stockholm: Wilhelm Hanson, 1968)

Northcott, Bayan, ed., *The Music of Alexander Goehr: Interviews and Articles* (London: Schott & Co., 1980)

O'Hagan, Peter, ed., *Aspects of British Music of the 1990s* (Aldershot: Ashgate, 2003)

Prausnitz, Frederik, *Score and Podium: A Complete Guide to Conducting* (New York: W. W. Norton & Co., 1983)

Rosen, Charles, *Schoenberg*, Fontana Modern Masters (London: Fontana, 1975)

Rudolph, Max, *The Grammar of Conducting: A Practical Guide to Baton Techniques and Orchestral Interpretation* (New York: Schirmer Books, 1980)

Samuel, Claude, *Conversations with Olivier Messiaen*, trans. Felix Aprahamian (London: Stainer & Bell, 1976)

Scherchen, Hermann, *Handbook of Conducting*, trans. M. D. Calvacoressi (London: Oxford University Press, 1935)

Schiff, David, *The Music of Elliott Carter* (London: Faber & Faber, 1998)

Smith Brindle, Reginald, *Contemporary Percussion* (London: Oxford University Press, 1970)

—— *The New Music: The Avant-garde since 1945* (London: Oxford University Press, 1975)

Steinitz, Richard, *Ligeti: Music of the Imagination* (London: Faber & Faber, 2003)

Stone, Else, and Kurt Stone, eds., *The Writings of Elliott Carter: An American Composer Looks at Modern Music* (Bloomington: Indiana University Press, 1977)

Stravinsky, Igor, *An Autobiography* (New York: W. W. Norton & Co., 1962)

—— *The Rite of Spring: Le Sacre du printemps: Sketches, 1911–1913: Facsimile Reproductions from the Autographs* (London: Boosey & Hawkes, 1969)

Stowell, Robin, ed., *The Cambridge Companion to the Cello* (Cambridge: Cambridge University Press, 1999)

Toff, Nancy, *The Development of the Modern Flute* (New York: Tablinger Publishing Co., 1979)

Tuckwell, Barry, *Horn*, Yehudi Menuhin Music Guides (London: Macdonald & Jane, 1983)

Turetzky, Bertram, *The Contemporary Contrabass* (Berkeley: University of California Press, 1979)

Varga, András Bálint, *Lutosławski Profile: Witold Lutosławski in Conversation with András Bálint Varga* (London: Chester Music, 1976)

Wagner, Richard, *On Conducting*, trans. Edward Dannreuther, 4th edition (London: William Reeves, 1940)

Wallace, John, and Alexander McGrattan, *The Trumpet* (New Haven, CT: Yale University Press, 2011)

Walsh, Stephen, *The Music of Stravinsky* (Oxford: Oxford University Press, 2000)

Waterhouse, William, *Bassoon*, Yehudi Menuhin Music Guides (London: Khan & Averill, 2005)

Wörner, Karl H., *Stockhausen: Life and Work*, trans. Bill Hopkins (London: Faber & Faber, 1973)

Index

PART ONE **Principles of technique**

Track 1   The baton
Eye-contact and alignment with the hand
Preparatory gesture
Independence of hands

PART THREE *Le Marteau sans maître*

Track 2   Three distinctive characteristics in conducting the work
(a) Irregular time units with varying metronome marks
(b) Plateau gesture and modification of irregular units
(c) Manner of controlling irregular units

Performance demonstrations

Track 3   Avant 'L'Artisanat furieux'
Track 4   Commentaire I de 'Bourreaux de solitude'
Track 5   L'Artisanat furieux'
Track 6   Commentaire II de 'Bourreaux de solitude'
Track 7   Bel édifice et les pressentiments, version première
Track 8   Après 'L'Artisanat furieux'
Track 9   Commentaire III de 'Bourreaux de solitude'
Track 10 Bel édifice et les pressentiments, double

Performers of *Le Marteau sans maître* examples on the DVD

The Warehouse Ensemble

Voice	Alison Wells
Flute	Nicholas Cartledge
Guitar	Jonathan Preiss
Viola	Rhiad Chibah
Xylophone	Matthew West
Vibraphone	Andrew Barclay
Percussion	Nicholas Reed
Conductor	Edwin Roxburgh